Dedication and Introduction

I'd like to dedicate this book to my wife Blanche, my children Kevin, Michael, Leilani, Alan, and Jennifer, and my precious grandchildren and great grandchildren. I owe the success I've had in my career to my family and to God in Heaven, and His Son, Jesus Christ.

This book is a recollection of the first four years of my 15-year career in the United States Navy, aboard my first ship, an ocean-going tugboat, the *U.S.S. Penobscot ATA-188.*

Many family members and friends have enjoyed listening to my experiences in the navy, but not in sequential order as presented here. The stories are all true, but a few names have been changed to protect privacy.

I thoroughly enjoyed my years in the navy. And I hope you'll also have fun reading these memories as I take you through *Life Aboard a Sinking Ship.*

Table of Contents

	Dedication and Introduction	Page	3
Chapter 1	How Did You End Up Here?	Page	5
Chapter 2	Qualifying for Officer's Training	Page	15
Chapter 3	Oil King	Page	21
Chapter 4	Serious Consequences	Page	27
Chapter 5	Shipmates	Page	35
Chapter 6	Have We Cleared the Channel?	Page	43
Chapter 7	Adventures and Misadventures	Page	47
Chapter 8	Troubles at Sea	Page	53
Chapter 9	Between Doldrums and Danger	Page	59
Chapter 10	Aboard a Sinking Ship	Page	65
Chapter 11	This is the Life!	Page	71
Chapter 12	A Beautiful Girl	Page	77
Chapter 13	What Now?	Page	83
Chapter 14	An Opportunity	Page	89
Chapter 15	An Accident and a Girl	Page	93
Chapter 16	Travel Troubles	Page	99
Chapter 17	A New Adventure	Page	107

Chapter 1

How Did You End Up Here?

The captain's eyes seemed to bore into each of us as the ship's entire crew stood silently on the deck. "I need a security crew onboard the ship!" he shouted. No one moved. No one volunteered.

Finally he barked, "Brown! Clauson! Yates! I want you to board her and make sure she doesn't go down!"

"Yes, Sir!" we said in unison.

The captain ordered the cook to give us a pot of strong coffee and a big plate of sandwiches. Handing us a two-way radio he said, "Stay on watch and let me know if she starts to sink again!"

Quickly the three of us scrambled over the side of our tugboat onto the deck of the disabled ship. I was glad the captain had chosen Boatswain Mate Brown. He and I were fairly good friends. I didn't know Metalsmith Clauson as well.

We sat down on the deck with our backs against the pilot house, and settled in as best we could in the bitter March wind. The tow cable jerked our ship forward as the *U.S.S. Penobscot ATA-188*, started up again. Every few minutes one of us went below deck to make sure there were no more leaks.

"So, Yates," Clauson asked, pulling his coat tightly around him. "How'd you end up here?" He reached out to warm his hands over the steaming pot of coffee. "I mean why did you join the Navy, and how'd you end up on an ocean-going tugboat like the *Penobscot*?"

"Well… " I hesitated. "It's a long story."

"No, really," Brown chimed in. "We have time to kill, and you've never told me much about your background. So how *did* you end up in the Navy?"

Brown was right. We had many hours ahead of us. Assuming the ship didn't spring another leak, we'd be talking to keep ourselves awake most of the night.

Thoughts raced through my mind. *How had I ended up here? … Why had I joined the Navy? …* The answer to those questions had really begun when I was just eight years old.

My first inkling of impending trouble came after the school bell rang on the cold morning of December 8, 1941. Miss Drohan, the teacher at our one-room schoolhouse in Liverpool, New York, called us to order, and then stood completely silent at the front of the classroom. She seemed frozen—like she had something very important to tell us, but didn't know where to begin. Usually, she smiled and greeted us, then we said the pledge of allegiance, and immediately started our classwork.

I wondered what was wrong. Had someone been hurt? Had somebody died? I stole a quick glance around the room to make sure everyone was there.

Finally, Miss Drohan took a deep breath, and said soberly, "Students, yesterday Pearl Harbor, in Hawaii, was bombed by the Japanese." She paused, "Many ships were sunk—and many lives were lost." Her voice trembled slightly as she continued, "And this morning President Roosevelt announced that our country is now at war."

Several students gasped. A dark mist of fear settled over our classroom. I felt like I couldn't breathe. Solemnly, we joined Miss Drohan in saying the pledge of allegiance. The words seemed to have a new, more profound, meaning.

At recess, instead of running outside to play, we stood around talking softly of what it meant to be at war. Would our country be attacked? Would our town?

Three days later Germany and Italy declared war on the United States. Newsreels showed men in battle and ships sinking. War suddenly became very real to me—and my world began to change. Quickly my father and I put up black-out curtains in all our windows. Everyone had to make sure there was no visible light outside during the night. That way, if enemy planes invaded, they would not be able to find the darkened cities. Within a few weeks we began to hear about neighbors and friends who had gone to war.

At night I lay in bed in the dark worrying that my father might have to go to war. After my mother left when I was four years old, my father hired care-givers to stay with me while he worked. The care-givers were sometimes mean and abusive. They beat me with a leather whip for the least infraction of their rules. I wondered what would happen to me if my father left. Finally, I mustered enough courage to ask him timidly, "Dad, will you have to go to war?"

"No, Billy," he said, calling me by my nickname. "I'm over 35 and have a family, so I won't be drafted in this horrible war!"

Soon it became difficult to buy certain supplies. In May of 1942, the government issued monthly ration books to everyone, based on the size of their families. The ration books contained removable stamps. Rationed items were only available if you had the right stamp. Gasoline, sugar, meat, cheese, milk, cooking fat, and canned goods were rationed.

At first the ration books were only for the two of us. But about a month after my 9th birthday, my father brought home a pregnant woman named Margaret, and said, "Billy, this is your new mother!" Soon baby Patricia was born. After that we got double ration books.

Margaret was not thrilled to have a ready-made 9-year-old stepson to take care of. And I didn't know how to relate to her. Along with my father's full-time job, he also leased 100 acres with a barn across the road from our house, where he raised animals and crops. I kept busy with chores on the farm and tried to stay out of Margaret's way.

The government called for farmers to help with the war effort by growing specific crops. At first, we grew corn, oats, and wheat. Later we added soybeans, which were used to make steering wheels for jeeps. We were also given burlap bags, called gunny sacks, that we filled with fluffy milkweed pods. These were used to stuff sleeping bags and life jackets.

As the war progressed, ration stamps were necessary to buy more things, such as coffee, shoes, bicycles, some fabrics, rubber, and more food items. I was glad we lived in the country and had a large garden, as well as cows, pigs, and chickens.

There were only 16 students in our little elementary school. It was easy to hear the lessons being taught to other grades. Miss Drohan allowed me to skip 3rd grade, and then 5th grade, since I already knew all the material.

I was 12 years old and a freshman in high school before World War II finally ended. We were all thrilled that the fighting was over! Black-out curtains were removed. Ration books were discontinued. We were free to buy whatever we could afford.

During my junior year of high school my mother remarried. She and her new husband went to court to get partial custody of me. The judge told me I must spend every other weekend with them in their home in Ithaca, New York, as well as the full month of August each year.

I was not happy to be spending time with my mother. My father had often told me she was a bad woman. He said she really didn't care for me, and that I needed to be very cautious around her.

Even though she was always kind to me on my weekend visits, I still felt ill at ease. I dreaded spending a whole month of August away from home! The first Sunday of August, I used the allowance money she gave me to buy a ticket for the two-hour bus ride back to my father's house in Liverpool. I called him and he gladly picked me up. We had a wonderful day together, but by afternoon my mother found out where I'd gone and told my father he'd have to send me back, or face legal consequences. My father took me to the bus station and paid for my ticket to Ithaca. He stood forlornly on the sidewalk watching as the bus pulled away from the depot.

My mother tried to make me feel more at home. When she found out I liked music, she quickly got me involved with singing in the large Methodist choir—which I thoroughly enjoyed. I flourished under the love and attention she lavished on me. Her husband, Clifford, was the Fire Chief at Ithaca Fire Station #5. A gentle and kind man, he made me feel welcome, and even bought me a used bicycle so I could more easily get around town.

I realized my father had been wrong. My mother was not a bad woman, and she loved me very much. She had actually taken me with her when she left my philandering father. It was my father who came and stole me away from her, and refused to let her see me when she tried to visit. By the end of August, although I missed my father, I made the decision to live with her full-time.

I'd always liked school. But the high school in Ithaca, New York, the home of Cornell University, was much more advanced than the one in Liverpool. Since I hadn't taken any math courses during my first three years of high school, I was told I needed to repeat 11th grade. I'd avoided math, because when I saw algebraic equations with letters and numbers, I was sure I would not be able to comprehend it. In Ithaca High School I found that math was actually fun and excelled in it! I continued to live with my mother for the rest of high school, and graduated in 1950, at the age of 17.

Just a few days after graduation, North Korea invaded South Korea. Within a few weeks American troops joined the battle. Once more our country was at war. I knew what that meant—and dreaded it! I expected to see rationing again. But this time there were no restrictions, since all the equipment for war had already been built, and supplies were stockpiled. America's only need was for men to fight the war in Korea. Soon friends and family members were being drafted.

I chose to take an extra year of high school so I could study more math. By the time I finished that year, the Korean War was in full swing. All men between the ages of 18 and 26 had to register for military duty, and were called up as needed. I turned 18 just before the end of my postgraduate year of high school. I went to the post office and filled out the paperwork to register—hoping I wouldn't be called to serve.

After high school I found a job in Rochester, New York. I planned to work long enough to save $800 for my first semester at Rochester Institute of Technology, where I'd been accepted as a mechanical engineering student. But I had no idea how to save money. I bought a top-quality multi-speed Raleigh bicycle from England (to save money on bus fare), an expensive watch, and a nice suit. I enjoyed my work and felt like I was on top of the world! Yet always lurking in the back of my mind was the thought that I might have to leave it all and go to war.

I'd been working in Rochester for over a year when I came back to my apartment one day, opened my mailbox, and saw an official-looking envelope. "Oh no!" I muttered. "This must be it!" Using my pocket knife to slit it open, I took out the letter and read, *Please report to . . .* I let out a long sigh. I was being drafted into the army.

I'd watched a newsreel of soldiers in Korea frantically digging foxholes while bullets shrieked overhead. I had no desire to dodge bullets or dig foxholes! So I made a quick trip to the navy recruiter's office.

When I showed the recruiter my draft notice, he said, "Son, you've come to the right place!" He rubbed his hands together and began his pitch—like a used-car salesman touting the wonders of an old jalopy. He assured me I'd be protected from the fighting if I joined the navy. The recruiter finished his presentation by pointing to the bright poster on the wall and reading it enthusiastically: "Join the Navy! See the World!"

The recruiter's spiel had been quite entertaining. "Well," I said, laughing, "if I have to be in the military anyway, I might as well *see the world!*"

- - - - - - - -

Brown and Clauson listened attentively as I told my story, making comments and laughing in all the right places. "So that's how I ended up in the Navy," I concluded.

But there is so much more to the story! I thought. I remembered how my stomach had begun to knot as I accepted the recruiter's proffered pen and signed my name.

Questions had raced through my mind. *How will I ever make it through boot camp? Where will I be sent? What kind of ship will I be stationed on? I'm not a good swimmer—will I be able to survive if I have to abandon ship? Will I <u>really</u> be able to stay out of combat?*

Chapter 2

Qualifying for Officer's Training

Even though I'd officially joined the navy, I didn't have to report for duty for two months, so I continued working for a few more weeks. Then I packed my belongings, stored them at my mother's house, and had time to say goodbye to friends and family.

On November 20, 1952, I took the bus to Buffalo, New York, where I reported to the induction center. There I was sworn in and issued an Armed Forces ID Card, as well as a set of "dog tags" (identification tags) to be worn on a chain around my neck. I was told that both of these were to be on me at all times, and if I should lose either, there would be serious consequences. Then I boarded the train bound for boot camp at Great Lakes Naval Training Center, north of Chicago.

It was midnight when I arrived at the Chicago station. Buses were waiting to take new recruits to boot camp. At the base I was assigned to a company of 60 men. It was about 2:00 a.m. before we were finally shown to our barracks by the chief petty officer who would be our company commander.

We were all exhausted. I quickly put on my pajamas and was about to climb into my bunk, when I realized the noisy chatter in the barracks had stopped. There was dead silence. I turned around to see what was wrong, and found 59 guys standing in their skivvies staring at me in my pajamas. I felt completely awkward and out of place. But I knew I'd look more foolish if I took off the pajamas right then, so I turned back and climbed into my bunk.

Three hours later reveille sounded at 0500 hours (5:00 a.m.). The chief petty officer came in shouting. He marched us to breakfast. After breakfast we were marched to the medical center to get physicals, shots, and have our heads shaved. Then we marched to a large well-organized warehouse. There, we were herded into a huge room lined with shelves, where attendants helped us pick out appropriate clothing and equipment. We were given sea bags (canvas duffel bags), military clothing (three of everything), shoes, and a ditty bag filled with toothbrush, toothpaste, comb, and shaving gear. They even had size 15 shoes to fit my feet. All clothes were stenciled with our names. Then we marched back to the barracks to put the contents of our seabags away in the small lockers by our bunks. After that we marched to lunch, and then on to the testing center. There we took tests to rate our IQs, mechanical abilities, math comprehension, and clerical skills. We were all totally worn out, and I found it difficult to think clearly during the tests. After that we marched back to the barracks where we were given boxes in which we were to pack our civilian clothes, to be shipped home. I included my pajamas.

Classes started early the next morning. Because of all the horror stories I'd heard, I was worried about the 12 weeks of boot camp. But I didn't find it difficult. We learned about navy terminology, military ranks, the parts and functions of different ships, knot-tying, semaphore signaling, and The Uniform Code of Military Justice. I paid attention, obeyed orders, and was at the top of my class. One day the company commander called me into his office. "Yates," he said, "you're doing very well. I'm appointing you as the Recruit Educational Petty Officer."

"Yes Sir!" I said, standing very straight and saluting. "What is a Recruit Educational Petty Officer, Sir?"

"That means you will help other recruits with their homework in the evenings."

"Yes, Sir. I'd be happy to do that, Sir!"

I also volunteered to be on the base drill team, doing precision marching for various ceremonies. I loved being part of that prestigious group.

A few weeks later our company commander again called me into his office. "Yates," he said. "The test results are in. You scored high enough to qualify for officers' training school. Congratulations!"

"Thank you, Sir!" I answered. "I'd be delighted to become an officer, Sir!"

"Well, you'll still need to take a few more tests," he added. "We'll get those scheduled right away."

Unfortunately, one of the tests revealed that I had some degree of color blindness. Naval officers need to be able to distinguish colored signal flags and lights, which are used when other means of communication are not available. I hadn't known I was slightly color blind. Sadly, it disqualified me from ever being a naval officer.

Every week a new company of sailors arrived. Midway through training, each company was assigned to a "service week," which included KP (kitchen) duty and grounds clean-up. Since I'd received the highest scores in all tests and classes, I was assigned to be the regimental messenger. I ran messages all over the base to various officers, waited while they wrote responses, and then carried them back. I relished striding outside in the fresh air instead of being confined to the kitchen or doing other manual labor.

Military ranks for enlisted men range from E1 (new recruits) up to E9 (Navy Master Chief Petty Officer—equivalent to an Army Master Sergeant). Responsibilities and pay increase with each advanced rating. At the end of boot camp we were upgraded to E2 (seaman apprentice) and given our orders. Some men from our company were going to Korea. Others were being sent to various ships or stations around the world. I breathed a sigh of relief when I saw that my assignment was for an ocean-going tugboat, the *U.S.S. Penobscot, ATA-188* in New York Naval Shipyard in Brooklyn—far from Korea! I was ordered to report in 10 days. A train ticket to New York—dated for that very day—was included with my orders.

Everyone in our company frantically packed their sea bags. Buses waited outside to take us to the train station. At the depot I had time to call my mother and tell her when I'd be arriving at Grand Central Station in New York City. She and my stepfather, Clifford, were there to meet me. They took me to their home for a few days. Then I rode a bus to my father's house, and from there back to Brooklyn.

I arrived at the base on Saturday, and was told the *Penobscot* was at sea and wouldn't be back until Monday. That night in the bunk at the receiving station I tossed and turned as thoughts raced through my mind. *I wonder what the tugboat will look like? How big will it be? How many guys will be stationed on it? Will I get seasick? Will I be able to remember everything I learned in boot camp?*

Chapter 3

Oil King

Monday afternoon I went down to the pier to witness the arrival of "my" ship. The *U.S.S. Penobscot* was machinery-gray in color, and resembled a typical toy tugboat a child might play with. The Ocean-Going Tug (Auxiliary) is not a large ship. It measures only about 130 feet in length. I was disappointed by the small size of the *Penobscot*. *Will I have to be stationed on this dinky little ship for the next four years?* I mused.

As it approached the pier, the sailors on deck called out for me to tie up the ship. They threw over the heavy rope, but I didn't know what to do. There's a *big* difference between book-learning, and actually tying up a ship in the real world! Seeing my hesitation, the leading boatswain mate uttered a few choice words, jumped to the dock, grabbed the rope, and tied up the ship. I was left standing there feeling humiliated. *So much for first impressions!*

As I went up the gangplank, I saluted ensign (flag) at the stern, and then saluted the officer of the deck, who was overseeing anyone boarding or leaving the ship. He examined my papers, and directed me to the personnel-man, where I turned in my orders. The personnelman showed me to the engineering crew compartment. There were four three-tiered bunks squeezed into a very small room. Each bunk looked to be two feet wide by six feet long. I knew my 6-foot 5½-inch frame would hang out the end. Only about two feet separated each bunk from the one above it. You couldn't sit up in bed. To get up you had to roll out and stand up. There was also a small locker for each sailor. I chose an empty middle bunk and began to unpack my sea bag.

The personnelman also gave me a liberty card. The purpose of the card was to regulate when a person could leave his duty station and enjoy a few hours (or days) off the ship. "If you lose your liberty card or your ID card, there will be serious consequences! It will mean an auto-matic two-week denial of liberty for each card. You'll be forced to stay aboard the ship during that time. And make sure," he added, "to keep all your belongings in your locker! The compartment cleaner is always on the lookout for 'gear adrift.' Anything found adrift will be confiscat-ed and put in the ship's safe until disciplinary action is completed."

I'd heard about the "serious consequences" at the induction center. I had no intention of losing my ID or liberty cards, and I planned to be especially careful not to leave anything out of my locker.

The next morning after breakfast, First Class Pet-ty Officer Corrigan, the lead engineer, came to get me.

"Come with me and I'll show you what your first job is."
He led me down to the engine room and handed me a
chipping hammer, paint scraper, and goggles, "I want you
to scrape all the paint off this big fire pump to prepare it
for repainting." He showed me how to do it and stated,
"I'll see you at noon in the mess hall!" He made it plain
that he did not want to see or hear from me until then. I
swallowed hard at the prospect of spending hours chipping paint. I knew it would be difficult and *very* boring
work. Corrigan saw my reaction. It seemed to please him.
"In fact," he continued with a sneer, "while we're at sea I
expect you to scape paint during the day whenever you're
not on duty!"

After lunch Corrigan came to show me around the
ship and tell me what my duties (besides scraping paint)
would be. "You'll be working in the engine room," he
said, "and you'll be the "Oil King."

"Oil king?" I queried.

"That means you'll be responsible for learning all
the piping and valves on the entire ship, and filling and
controlling all of the fluids, including diesel fuel, lubri-
cating oil, salt water for cooling the engines, fresh water,
and steam."

"Yes, sir!" I said, wondering just how I was going to
do all that.

Corrigan continued the tour. "Here'a the peak tank
that holds fresh water." he said, gesturing toward the
huge pie-shaped tank in the bow (front) of the ship. "Up
here is the galley storage," he nodded toward a storeroom
above the peak tank. I could see dry goods such as cereal,

flour, pasta, and canned goods. "And here," he pointed to a small room just aft of (behind) the peak tank, "is the Quartermaster's storeroom." I nodded my head and peeked in. I could see sextants, and other expensive navigation equipment, along with numerous navigation maps. Next came the officer's quarters, and then the mess hall in the middle of the ship.

I started my work as the oil king immediately. I knew I must map out the piping throughout the entire ship and locate the valves for controlling various liquids. As I removed deck plates and learned the color coding and routing of the different pipes, I became *very* well acquainted with the *Penobscot*.

Our first trip out to sea was the once-a-month kitchen-garbage run for the entire naval shipyard. As we passed Montauk Point on Long Island, I started feeling queasy. I rushed to the rail, leaned over, and threw up. I had to go back to work in the engine room, but was unable to eat the rest of the day. After we sailed several more hours, they dumped the garbage off the garbage scow we were towing, and headed back to port. That was the only time I ever got seasick.

Our next trip out was a rather long one, and all the fresh water tanks were almost empty when we returned. My task was to refill them using a 1½-inch fire hose connected to the fresh water tap on the dock. This was the first time I was required to fill the forward peak tank, which held tens of thousands of gallons of fresh water.

I dragged the fire hose aboard the ship, threaded it down through the hatch on the weather deck, through another hatch on the main deck, and into the tank. Then I climbed back to the dock and turned on the water valve. It was midmorning when I started filling the tank. At first I checked the water level every hour. Nothing much seemed to be happening. By mid-afternoon the tank was less than ¼ full. I checked again at suppertime and found it was still less than half full.

After supper they always showed a movie in the mess hall, which lasted about 1½ hours. It had two reels that had to be changed halfway through the movie. Since I knew the peak tank wouldn't be full until the middle of the night, I planned to check it after the movie. As we watched the film, the men began having difficulty staying seated on the mess hall benches. When the movie operator turned on the light to change the reel, the officer of the day looked up the passageway and bellowed, "Yates! Why are there cereal boxes floating down the passageway past my cabin?!"

"Oops!" I shouted. Bounding off the bench, I scrambled through the door onto the deck, leaped from the ship to the dock, and hurriedly turned off the valve. The bow of the ship was almost submerged in the water. I had not only filled the peak tank, but also the navigation compartment, as well as most of the dry storage compartment. The food was waterlogged and the maps were floating. Fortunately, the officers' quarters doors were shut and did not get flooded. The officer commanded the damage control team (really the ship's entire crew) to man the pumps to get rid of the excess water from the compartments.

"I don't understand," I told the officer. "It took all day to fill less than half the tank!"

"Well, I know exactly what happened!" he exclaimed.

Chapter 4

Serious Consequences

S o what did I do wrong to cause it to flood like that?" I asked, picking up a waterlogged map with two fingers and tossing it onto the growing pile on the dock.

"It wasn't you," the officer exclaimed, shaking his head. "It was the yard birds!"

"Yard birds?" I questioned.

"After the yard birds finished work and went home," he said, using the nickname for shipyard workers, "all the water from the entire dock started feeding into our little fire hose. When that happens, the pressure jumps about five times higher. So your tank was full within a few minutes and the water kept pouring in."

The officer understood that I hadn't known about the pressure differential of day versus night, so I wasn't disciplined. But he gave me a serious tongue-lashing, ending with, "You need to watch out for this in the future!" Then he shook his head and mumbled incredulously, "We must have taken on an extra 20,000 gallons of water!"

It was actually good training for the crew, since

they rarely had an emergency where they had to man the pumps. We finally got things under control around midnight. We never did get to see the rest of the movie we'd been watching.

One morning I inadvertently left my wallet on my bunk during breakfast. I didn't realize what I'd done until Compartment Cleaner Jackson, grinned triumphantly at me and said, "Hey Yates! I wrote you up for leaving your ID and liberty cards out! That's four weeks with no liberty!" He walked away looking very pleased with himself.

Oh no! I thought. *What have I done? I can't believe I forgot!* I dreaded a whole month without being able to leave the ship.

The following morning the captain announced we were going to Bermuda and would be staying there for a day. I just hung my head. This was my first opportunity to be out of the continental United States, and I'd blown it!

The trip to Bermuda was uneventful. The island looked vibrantly beautiful as we pulled into port. I watched as the other sailors left to go on liberty. The men came back later in the day laughing and happy, bragging about their exploits. While I was off duty, all I could do was sit on deck and gaze longingly at the shore. I was glad when we finally pulled away from the islands and headed back toward Brooklyn!

When my four weeks were up, I went to the personnelman and asked for my wallet back. He told me it had never been turned in. Jackson feigned ignorance. He said he had no idea what had happened to my wallet. I was fairly sure he'd pocketed the money and tossed the wallet overboard. That meant I had to get my ID card and liberty card, as well as my driver's license, replaced. It took several more weeks before everything was in order, and I could finally leave the ship for some much-needed liberty.

A few days later while I was in the shower, I realized I was wearing the expensive wrist watch I'd bought while working in Rochester. I didn't want to get dressed and take it back to my locker, so I reached across the passageway and laid it on a shelf. I could see over the shower curtain and thought it would be safe. Just before I got out of the shower, Jackson walked through the passageway. When I was done toweling off, I reached for my watch. The shelf was empty!

I dressed quickly and went to confront Jackson. He innocently said he hadn't seen it. But he was the only one who had gone through the head (bathroom area) while I was showering. There was no way to prove anything, but after that I became extremely careful to make sure my belongings were properly stowed in my locker.

Sometime later I was working on a piece of equipment in the mess hall while Jackson was sitting at one of the tables reading a magazine. I needed a different tool and ran down to the engine room to get it. It took less than a minute, but when I returned, the long screwdriver I'd laid on the table was gone. "Jackson! Did you take my screwdriver?" I asked.

"No. I haven't seen it!" he replied. Then he closed his magazine, got up, stretched, and sauntered toward the door. I could see the outline of my screwdriver in his back pocket under his shirt.

I quickly stepped forward, yanked up his shirt and snatched the screwdriver from his pocket. "You thief!" I yelled. "You've been stealing things from me since I got here!" Jackson just shrugged and walked away.

Except for Jackson, most the men onboard the *Penobscot* were nice fellows. I became close friends with several of them as we spent time working, talking, and going on liberty together. They invited me to the USO (United Service Organization) dances on Saturday nights at the local YMCA. I declined because I didn't know how to dance. With my big feet I was sure I'd trip up any partner!

A few months after I'd gotten my liberty card back, I was thrilled when the captain announced we were going to Bermuda again. I was especially careful to make sure all my belongings were safely in my locker! I didn't want to miss out this time. It was raining hard when we docked at the island, but I couldn't wait to get ashore. My friend Boatswain Mate Brown and I decided to go sightseeing and shopping together. We wanted to see everything! Just as we stepped off the gangplank the clouds parted and the tropical sun seemed to welcome us.

We explored the colorful little outdoor shops in the marketplace where hawkers tried to convince us we desperately needed to spend our money on their goods. Then we followed the sound of music over to a roped-off grassy area where couples were dancing to the beat of Latin rhythms. They were really good! It was fun to watch them dip and twirl. The crowd of onlookers clapped appreciatively when the music stopped.

Suddenly a man leaned in close to my ear and asked loudly, "Do you like to dance" His question made me jump.

"Uh, no! I don't know how to dance," I replied, stepping back.

"Then you should come right over here!" He grabbed my arm and pulled me toward a colorful display with brochures and pictures of beautiful women dancing with handsome men. "What you need is some Arthur Murray dance lessons! You'd be a natural!" He went on to tell me how easy it would be for me to learn to dance like a pro, and how smooth it would make me with the ladies.

Brown snickered, "Yeah, Yates! You need to learn how to move those big feet of yours, so you can go with us to the USO dances in Brooklyn."

Seeing my hesitation, the salesman added the clincher, "Brooklyn! Why, you can take your classes right near your home base. And since you are a serviceman, I can give you a discount if you sign up today!"

I wondered if I could ever *really* learn to dance smoothly. But if Arthur Murray classes would make it happen, then I was willing to give it a try! I shelled out the money and signed up for 20 lessons.

Brown and I headed back to the ship late that evening with our bellies full and our wallets empty. It had been a satisfying day! My head was swirling with the bright colors, smells, tastes and sounds of the beautiful tropical island.

Naval assignments for the *Penobscot* were varied. Sometimes we towed loaded barges up and down the

Eastern Seaboard, and occasionally a small "moth-balled" navy ship that was being recommissioned. We never knew if we'd be given specific orders once a week, or once a month. At times we'd be away from our base for several months. We towed navy ships ranging in size from Navy Yard Tugs (some less than 100 feet long) to Navy Escort Destroyers (450 to 500 feet). The yard tugs came in three sizes: YTL (yard tug little), YTM (yard tug medium), and YTB (yard tug big). They were used for towing within the naval shipyard, whereas our ocean-going tugboat had a steel hull and was built to withstand ocean navigation.

As I worked in the engine room, I became more and more experienced at repairing and maintaining the equipment. The ship's continual vibration, and the constant bucking of the waves at sea, caused the engine cylinder liners to wear out regularly. While we were in our berth at Brooklyn Naval Yard, we worked on preventative maintenance. But because we might be called at any time to do a job at sea, we could only overhaul one cylinder at a time. There were 12 cylinders in each of the two main engines. I became proficient at dismantling, checking, and replacing the cylinder liners.

I also worked on the steam boiler, which regularly loosened under the strain of ocean currents, causing diesel fuel to leak. As I tightened and adjusted the fuel fittings, I became familiar with the engine room spare parts, so Corrigan put me in charge of inventorying and ordering spare parts.

I got to know my two watch-mates in the engine

room quite well. It was impossible to carry on a normal conversation there, because of the huge engines roaring in our ears. If you needed to communicate, you used hand gestures, shouted directly into the other person's ear, or stuck your head in the box sitting on the desk with an opening at one end, called the "dog house," which had a phone inside. It cut out a lot of the engine noise and was wide enough for two people to put their heads into the enclosure to communicate.

Early one morning Johnson, the electrician of the watch (whom we called Sparkey), signaled excitedly for me to come over to the dog house. "Okay!" I shouted and headed there.

Chapter 5

Shipmates

Sparkey and I stuck our heads inside the dog house. "Hey, Yates," Sparkey said. "Do you see that fly over there on the bulkhead?" He pointed to the port-side (left) wall. "Over on the bulkhead there's a big old fly. Do you see it?"

I wondered how a fly could have gotten into the engine room, since we were at sea and had not stopped in a port for several days. But I pulled my head out of the dog house and looked where he'd indicated. I didn't see anything, so I leaned back in. "I don't see any fly, Sparkey. Where is it?"

"It's right over there," he said, swinging his arm excitedly. "Look! See if you can see it!"

Again I pulled my head out, looked, and then stuck my head back in. "Sorry, but I can't seem to see any fly, Sparkey. Can you *really* see a fly over there?"

"I don't see it either," he said solemnly. Pausing for effect, he continued, "But I hear it walking around!" I just shook my head.

Sparkey was responsible for everything electrical in

the engine room while we were underway. He operated the propulsion stand, adjusting outputs of the generators, and monitoring the current being drawn by the main propulsion motors.

One day a voltmeter on the port-side engine stopped working. Since we were underway and couldn't get the meter fixed or replaced, Sparkey had to take a manual reading at least once every hour. Each time he went over to the engine generator, opened a little hatch, balanced an expensive meter on the handrail, took two leads and touched the proper spots on the side of the generator to check the voltage. If the voltage was not correct, he had me adjust a knob at the propulsion stand to get the voltage to read 500 volts on his meter.

I watched Sparkey do this many times. By then I was the petty officer of the watch. I had learned a lot about engines, pumps, centrifuges, governors, and all kinds of things mechanical and hydraulic—even how to overhaul an entire engine. I thought, *I'm now the leader of the engine room on our watch, and I should know how to take the meter readings.* So I said, "Sparkey can I take the reading this time?"

"Oh, sure!" he said. Do you know how to do it?"

"Yes, I've watched you do it numerous times."

I took the meter, set it carefully on the handrail, took the leads and reached out to touch the correct spots. I touched the first spot, then as the second probe made contact, everything exploded. The leads blew out of my hands. The meter burst into a giant fireball, and crashed to the deck in pieces.

Sparkey rushed over shouting, "Are you okay?!"

"Yeah, I'm fine," I said, shakily. "But I don't understand what just happened!"

He picked up the pieces of the meter, looked at them and said, "Hey! You've got it set on Ohms! You have to set it on DC volts before you take a voltage reading, not Ohms!"

"What are Ohms?" I said, looking at him blankly. I felt like a complete idiot. This meter cost over $800. Fortunately, since there were three different watch teams, they had another meter on board we could borrow.

Right then I realized that although I knew quite a bit about a lot of things, I knew nothing about electricity. I made a mental note to somehow rectify that as soon as possible.

First Class Petty Officer Corrigan was in charge of overseeing the entire engine room. He was a veteran of World War II. Although he was somewhat knowledgeable, he continually bragged about his abilities. He tended to be churlish and snapped at everyone, letting us know that he was the ultimate "salty" sailor, who knew all there was to know about everything. He considered the rest of us lowly peons. He was not well-liked by the crew in general, but the engineers especially despised his overbearing know-it-all attitude.

The engine room was about 40 feet long and 30 feet wide. Two large General Motors engines which supplied power to the screw (propeller), jutted into the center of the space. Next to each of them was an auxiliary engine which powered the generator that provided electricity for the ship. A 5-foot-wide reduction gear filled the center of the room, with an 8-inch shaft, which powered the screw, protruding from the reduction gear.

In the aft end of the engine room, on the starboard (right) side, there was a short ladder going up to a 6-by-12-foot platform, called the half deck, which extended close to the steering gear in the middle of the room. Corrigan didn't like to sleep in the engineering compartment, so he set up his sleeping cot on the half deck next to the workbench. Since he was responsible for all the maintenance of the engine room, Corrigan didn't have regular watches. But he was usually doing something on the half deck. Since he was fairly anti-social, he didn't like going to the mess hall any more than necessary. While we were at sea, he set up a hot plate on the workbench. He often made mulligan stew and ate that for several meals. In rough seas he had a difficult time trying to keep the hot plate and pot of stew on the workbench. So he used ropes and other equipment to keep the hot plate wedged securely in place.

One day while I was on watch, the ship suddenly lurched to port. The hotplate stayed in place, but the pot of stew flew into the huge steering gear where it caught in the chain that controls the ship's rudder, and crumpled like a piece of wadded aluminum foil. The stew splattered over the half deck. Furious and disgusted, Corrigan screamed out profanities, and shouted for us to come help him clean up the mess.

One morning at sea, after I finished my morning watch and had breakfast, I went out on deck to get some fresh air. Suddenly I heard a loud roar. Startled, I quickly turned toward the sound. Thick black smoke was pouring from the ship's funnel. Within another minute the roar came again, and more black smoke billowed out. I rushed down to the engine room to see what was happening.

"What's going on?" I asked Second Class Petty Officer Baker, who was in charge of that watch.

"The auxiliary engine just ran away and wouldn't stop accelerating! I'm not sure, but the governor may have failed. The only way I was able to shut down the engine was by wrapping a heavy coat around the air intake, cutting off the oxygen supply. Corrigan insisted on taking the governor, which he thinks is bad." He pointed toward Corrigan, who stood on the half deck tearing the governor apart.

"Wait a minute!" I said. "That's a factory-only repair item. He's not allowed to do that!"

"I know. But you know how he is. There's no reasoning with him," Baker said. "Go get me another governor out of spares."

I knew right where to get another governor. Baker installed it on the engine to see if that would cure the problem. He started the engine, which immediately began to rev up and run away. He used the coat again to smother the air intake and stop the engine.

"I don't think it's the governor!" Baker said, turning toward me. "It must be something else." I agreed with him.

Meanwhile Corrigan heard the commotion and yelled, "Yates, get another governor out of spares! There must be two bad governors!"

Baker and I looked at each other and shook our heads. We knew that was not possible. It *had* to be something else. We started taking apart the governor drive-gear from the engine to see if we could find the problem.

The shaft assembly coming out of the engine (which drives the governor) consisted of two parts. A bevel gear coupled the horizontal to the vertical shafts. We took the gear housing off the engine, and pulled the shaft and gear assembly out. The gear had worn completely smooth. The problem was in the drive gear—not the governor. I found another shaft and gear assembly in spare parts, and we installed it.

While we were working on the gear assembly, Corrigan grabbed the second governor, took it up to the workbench, and started to dismantle it. I knew there was a third governor in spare parts, so I went and got that. We installed it and started the engine. It worked perfectly.

Corrigan heard the engine running properly and yelled down to us, "Finally! We got a good governor!"

Baker and I looked at each other and shrugged. We didn't bother explaining to Corrigan what the problem was. He wouldn't have believed us anyway.

While we were in port, all the sailors had quite a bit of free time. Although some jobs required more work than others, everyone had off at least every third weekend. A few of the deck crew got together and went to bars whenever they had a night off at the same time. They all owned cars, so they took turns driving to one of their favorite bars in the residential section of Brooklyn. There they drank, told stories, and flirted with any girls who came in. After a couple of hours, they'd move to another of their familiar haunts and continue drinking. When they got tired of that place, they would go on to another one.

By the time they reached the third bar, they were so inebriated they had trouble finding a parking place with plenty of room so they wouldn't need to parallel park. They stayed at that bar until it closed in the wee hours of the morning. Then they'd stumble outside—so polluted they could rarely remember where they'd parked. Sometimes they found the car and tried to cautiously inch their way back to the ship without hitting anyone or anything. Other times, when they couldn't find the car, they hired a taxi to take them back to the ship. I often heard them laughing and saying they'd lost the car again. On their next night off another man would drive his car. They weren't worried about finding their cars, because after several days the police would pick up the abandoned car and tow it to the police compound. The sailors checked the police lot periodically and paid $12 each to get their cars out of hock. I was not part of the drinking crowd and normally didn't go to the bars.

While we were out on our trips, the 33 men onboard our tugboat were divided into three watches: sections one, two, and three (four hours on and eight hours off). Living in such tight quarters meant we *really* got to know each other. It brought out the best—and worst—in the men. One sailor, Second Class Quartermaster Presley, was an amiable guy, and very capable, but he had one recurring problem that kept getting him into trouble.

Chapter 6

Have We Cleared the Channel?

One night while we were in port, I had the mid-watch in the engine room from midnight to 0400 hours. It wasn't necessary for me to stay in the engine room during the entire time; I only had to check every few minutes to make sure things were running smoothly. So I was sitting in the mess hall reading, when Quartermaster Presley stumbled in dragging a bicycle he'd lifted from one of the yard birds. Presley liked to drink, and that night he'd obviously been at it all evening. He was hardly able to stand, let alone maneuver a bicycle.

Angry about something, Presley gave the front tire of the bike a good kick. He became more and more agitated and continued to loudly voice his displeasure. As his anger escalated, he hammered down the front fender with his foot, He began to rant incoherently as he destroyed the wheels, smashed both fenders, and bent the frame.

"Presley!" I shouted, "What *are* you doing? You can't just take someone's bike and destroy it! You're going to get in big trouble when they find it!"

Presley blinked at me in owlish confusion. He hadn't

even noticed I was there. Comprehension slowly began to spread across his face. In a slurred voice he said, "Yur rrright!" Dragging the bicycle outside, he lifted it over the gunwale, and heaved it into the water. I stood there in utter disbelief as he turned and staggered unsteadily toward his bunk.

Another time, after we picked up a barge at Mayport Basin in Florida, we had "Cinderella Liberty," which meant we had to be back at the ship by midnight in preparation for leaving early the following morning. The captain had assigned Presley with the responsibility for taking the ship out of port.

We were to leave Mayport Basin that particular morning around 0600. I had the morning watch that day (0400 to 0800) in the engine room. At 0600 hours Presley called down and asked if we were ready to get underway. The engine room crew included three men: the petty officer of the watch (me), the electrician, who took care of the actual propulsion of the ship by turning dials at his propulsion stand, and the wiper, a sailor of lower rank who wiped up any oil spills, and took readings on the various meters and gauges every half hour, recording them in a log. The three of us signaled that we were ready.

Presley said, "Let's go!" He ordered ⅓ speed, so we cranked up the dials to get the propeller shaft going at ⅓ speed. Everything seemed okay, but the ship felt a little different than usual. We assumed the water must be rough. Soon Presley ordered ⅔ speed. We cranked her up to ⅔ speed. Then suddenly he ordered "STOP!"

That's weird. I thought. *You don't stop a ship in the*

middle of a narrow channel. We could hit the side of the channel! Something must be wrong!

I rushed topside, and found quite a drama unfolding on the bridge. Presley had been drinking the night before, and hadn't gotten much sleep before his watch. He was unsteady on his feet, and his brain was still pickled. He'd struggled to even make it to the bridge. About the time he had signaled us to go ⅔ speed, the captain was jarred awake. He ran up to the bridge and shouted, "Presley, what in tarnation are you doing?!"

Presley slurred, "Have we cleared the channel yet, Cap'n?"

"Cleared of the channel?" the captain bellowed. "Presley, we're still tied up to the pier! Stop the engines immediately!" Presley had forgotten to tell the deck crew to untie the ship. The captain shook his head as he said, "Presley, get below and get some sleep!"

I don't know whether he got in trouble for that escapade or not. Sometimes Presley was a second class petty officer, and other times he would be demoted to third class petty officer because of his antics. He was bright, and good at his job, so after a while he'd get enough points, score well on tests, and acquire a high enough recommendation to get back up to second class status. Then he'd goof up—usually because of his drinking—and get reduced in rank again to third class. Presley's problems were of his own making. I felt sorry for him. But after I'd been aboard ship a few months, I had a problem of *my* own making. It started one afternoon while we were at sea.

Chapter 7

Adventures and Misadventures

While we were away from our home port, part of my work as the ship's oil king was to continually watch the levels of the diesel fuel which was stored in three midship tanks: a large one in the middle, with a smaller saddle tank on each side. Each saddle tank had a deck-level vent so the air above the fuel could escape as the tank filled.

One Saturday while we were at sea, I noticed the port saddle tank was getting low on fuel, which meant I needed to transfer some from the center tank. I went to the engine room and turned on the pump to start transferring fuel.

Since I knew it would take quite a while, I headed to the mess hall for lunch. After we finished lunch that day the crew stayed in the mess hall to watch one of movies we brought onboard before we sailed. As we were watching the movie, the bottom of the screen became more and more out of focus. Everyone grumbled, but that sometimes happened when the sea was rolling a certain way.

Suddenly, with a start, I remembered that I was

transferring fuel—and hadn't checked the levels in the last hour! I got up quietly and made my way toward the door. As I opened the door to the deck, I saw fuel gushing out of the port side vent into the ocean. The tank was so full the ship was listing to the port side. That explained why the movie was out of focus! I hurriedly closed the door, and almost tripped over my feet as I spun around and rushed down to the engine room. I shut off the fuel transfer pump and reversed the flow, so the fuel would pump back into the center tank. I don't know how many thousands of gallons had spilled overboard—but it was a significant amount!

Then I tiptoed back to the mess hall. Everyone was still watching the movie, so no one suspected what was happening. By the time the film was over, the ship was finally on an even keel again—with the fuel properly distributed between the tanks. I breathed a sigh of relief. But I felt like such a fool for not paying attention to what I was doing. I couldn't believe I forgot I was transferring fuel!

My problems were not resolved, though, because every day I had to take a depth sounding of how much fuel was left in each tank and record the figures in a log for the engineering officer. If I recorded the exact amount of fuel left in the tanks, I would have been in big trouble because of the major drop in fuel levels. My mistake could result in serious disciplinary action—with at least a demotion in rank. It was also possible that we might run out of fuel before we got back to port, which would be very serious. We could end up dead in the water with no electrical power—perhaps even unable to signal for help.

I laid awake in my bunk that night trying to figure out just what to do. I hadn't intended to forget that I was transferring fuel. I was *so* ashamed of my negligence! But my remorse would not hold up if I were to be court-marshaled.

The next day I went out on deck and opened the caps at the top of each fuel tank, as I'd always done. I let down the weighted steel tape into the tank that I used to calculate the level of fuel. After pulling the tape out, I wrote down the fuel level, and went to record the figures in the log. I knew approximately how much fuel we normally used daily from each tank, so I subtracted a percentage off each total amount of fuel on hand, and recorded the false readings.

Every day I adjusted the figures a bit more. I was riddled with guilt over my falsehood, and continually worried we might not make it back to port. I breathed a huge sigh of relief when we pulled safely into our berth in Brooklyn—with fuel still on hand. By then the levels in the fuel log were finally accurate. No one questioned why the ship had used so much more fuel on that trip. No one ever suspected or asked. And I, of course, did not tell.

I loved being in the Navy. I appreciated the experience and knowledge I'd acquired. And I reveled in the friendship of my mates. I'd never before experienced the camaraderie I had with the other sailors on the *Penobscot*. We were together 24/7. Through the dangers we'd faced, the fun, and even the crazy times, we'd become a family. My carelessness had jeopardized everyone's safety. I never wanted that to happen again!

On our next trip out at sea I was *especially* vigilant in my role as the oil king. I was determined to do the best job possible in all my work. A few days into our voyage the captain announced that we'd be stopping overnight in Puerto Rico. I'd read quite a bit about Puerto Rico, so I was looking forward to visiting that beautiful Island.

I was waiting on deck when we pulled into the naval base at the Port of Roosevelt Roads. Brilliant turquoise water lapped softly on the nearby white sand beaches lined with palm trees. After they lowered the gangplank, my friend Sparkey and I were the first sailors off the ship. We quickly headed for the long row of taxis that were lined up like hungry sharks, waiting for prey. As we climbed into the first taxi in line, the driver revved his engine. We asked him to take us to the nearest town. Without a word he slammed his foot down on the gas pedal. Sparkey whispered, "I think this guy thinks he's a racecar driver—and he just heard the starting gun!"

The driver never let up on the gas as we bounced through potholes and careened around corners. Within 20 minutes we arrived at Fajardo, a beautiful port city on the eastern coast of Puerto Rico. The taxi finally screeched to a halt at the town square. Grateful to have survived the wild ride, we paid the driver and climbed out.

After straightening our rumpled uniforms and adjusting our caps, we looked around. The taxi had deposited us at the edge of a large square park with lush lawns dotted with flowers and trees. Businesses surrounded the park on all sides. I'd heard that this style was typical of many

Spanish towns. Sparkey and I wandered around the shops, buying a few trinkets to send home.

Late in the afternoon we saw Puerto Rican young people start to gather in the park. The young men began to walk around the park in one direction, and girls, walking in groups, strolled the opposite way. Although there were no couples, we could see lots of flirting happening as the groups passed each other.

"So, do you want to join the parade?" Sparkey asked as we watched.

"Sure, why not!" I replied.

We joined the young men walking counter clockwise. The girls in colorful dresses, with bright flowers in their hair, smiled and sent coy glances our way. We walked for almost an hour. By then a few other sailors from our ship had joined the parade.

Finally we stopped to get a bite to eat at a tiny restaurant where we sat at tables outside facing the park. After that we checked out a few more shops. Just before dark, we hailed another taxi and headed back to the ship. This time the driver was in no hurry, and we could enjoy the beautiful scenery.

I sighed contentedly as I climbed into my bunk, and went to sleep dreaming of future adventures in more new and exciting places.

During my first two years on the *Penobscot*, we made many trips up and down the east coast of the United States. Along with visiting Puerto Rico, and periodically going to Bermuda (which was always fun!), we stopped by Guantanamo Bay in Cuba for one day. I could see the surrounding steep hills dotted with tropical foliage as I went ashore. We'd been told that we could not leave the Navy base. So I wandered around the base and got a sandwich for lunch. Then I spent some time standing on the dock watching the brightly colored boats that were tied up to the Navy pier. The boats were full of bananas of varying sizes, shapes, and colors. I never dreamed there were so many types of bananas! Sailors stopped by the boats to buy hands of bananas.

I loved seeing new places and was hoping we'd be sent to Canada. But it wasn't until January of second year on the *Penobscot* when we were finally ordered to go up the western coastline of Newfoundland, Canada, to pick up a barge with a very large crane anchored on its deck. It was a bitterly cold winter, not exactly the ideal time to be going north toward the arctic circle. I hoped the crane would be well-secured!

Chapter 8

Troubles at Sea

Night had just fallen when we arrived in Newfoundland. It took over an hour to get the crane loaded and ready to go. Then we headed south through the Gulf of St. Lawrence, toward Sydney, Nova Scotia. We planned to spend a day in Sydney's large protected harbor before heading northeast to deliver the barge to Argentia, Newfoundland.

Almost immediately after getting back out to sea we started encountering ice floes—which are large piles of floating ice, like minature icebergs. Since it was dark, the helmsman couldn't see to avoid the ice floes. I was in my bunk trying to sleep, but every few minutes we'd ram into an ice floe and hear a big *clunk!* and then *bang! bang! bang!* as the ice scraped along both sides of the hull. Soon we'd hit another, and the ship would again rock and bump. There was no way anyone could sleep. This continued most of the way to Nova Scotia. By 0200 hours we finally anchored in the calm waters of Sydney's harbor where we could all get some rest at last.

The next morning I awoke to total silence. Hurriedly

I dressed and bounded up the ladder to the deck. A light fog covered the harbor as I gazed out on a sea that looked like it was made of solid glass. We were totally iced in! The provincial authorities ordered a Canadian icebreaker to clear a path for us, but it took two days for the icebreaker to arrive and free us. In the meantime, we played cards and acey-deucy (a form of backgammon) between watches.

We stood on deck and cheered as the icebreaker finally plowed its way through the ice. The ship left a clear channel—just wide enough for us to safely navigate out of the harbor. We were hardly out of sight of land when we ran into one of those infamous North Atlantic winter storms, with high winds and huge waves. The going was slow. No matter how we tried to avoid it, the ship kept getting caught sideways to the waves. We'd roll 45° degrees to port and then 50° to starboard, for a total roll of 95°. No one could sleep. You couldn't stay in the bunk unless you lashed yourself down, and even then the rolling still made it impossible to get any rest. We didn't dare undress, in case we had to abandon ship.

The radio reports said we were headed directly into the storm. The waves were 20-30 feet high and increasing. On the second day the captain decided we'd better head back to Sydney and wait out the storm there. He turned the ship around in a big arc—being careful not to foul the barge tow cable—and we headed back toward Sydney.

Unfortunately, it appeared that instead of getting out of the storm, we were heading into it. It got worse and worse, so the captain finally turned around again and we continued toward our goal of Argentia. He didn't realize that the storm was going the same speed we were. It was a rough trip! The exterior of the ship became heavily coated with ice. The deck was so slick that no one could keep their footing and stand up on it.

Eating was extremely difficult. The galley cooks couldn't prepare a full hot meal. They put soup in a large cauldron and gave each sailor a bowl of soup and a sandwich. You had to hold the sandwich in your hand, put the soup on top, and try to balance. It was challenging to stand up in the mess hall, but it was *impossible* to sit down. We ended up standing and rolling with the ship—like a row of metronomes slowly rocking from side to side—trying to stay upright. I desperately struggled to balance as I took each spoonful, finishing the soup first, before eating the sandwich. Once in a while someone would spill their soup, so the mess hall deck started to became quite slippery. Then the fun really began!

At lunch on the third day of this hazardous journey, I was just wolfing down the last bite of my sandwich when Boatswain Mate Andrews, a tough sailor who'd been in the Navy for over 20 years and was considered a seasoned salt, came into the galley. He collected his bowl of soup, a spoon, and a sandwich. Turning to walk away, he lost his footing on a greasy spot and started sliding. As the ship began its starboard roll, he slid downhill and ended up hitting the starboard door with a bang. The bowl exploded and shards of glass flew all over the mess hall deck. Andrews stood there for a minute, looking from the soggy sandwich in his hand to the shattered glass every-where. Suddenly his face crumpled and he began to wail and cry big crocodile tears.

The fatigue and tension of the last few days were taking their toll. We were all exhausted! Everyone was having problems eating—everyone, that is, who could eat. Many of the crew members were so sick from the ship's movements they had no desire for food.

The trip that should have taken a day or two, stretched into five days before we reached Argentia. It was evening when we finally pulled into the protect-ed harbor to deliver the barge. The fog was so thick I couldn't see the dock. Two of our three duty sections were allowed to pull liberty and stay out until midnight. There was a bar nearby and the sailors headed there to warm up and relax.

I needed to stay onboard because the fresh water tanks had to be filled. I was exhausted and frustrated, but the tanks must be full for our return trip. Icy fingers of bitter cold crept in under my heavy clothing, chilling me to the bone. I finally finished around midnight—just in time to see the sailors coming back. The men had been so worn out and distraught that once they hit the warm, dimly-lit bar, they couldn't stop drinking. Quite a few had to crawl aboard and one was carried.

The next morning when we headed back toward Brooklyn Naval Sdhipyard, I was one of the few without a hangover. For once I was glad I'd been forced to stay aboard the ship!

A few months after our trip to Newfoundland, I was

sent to a three-day refrigeration course at the New York Naval Ship Yard. I learned about the refrigeration cycle, and all the various parts and valves within the refrigeration piping system.

The York one-ton refrigeration system on our ship fed refrigerant to our two big walk-in units—one was a cooler for vegetables, and the other a meat freezer. Most of the detailed maintenance was performed by a maintenance man from York Corporation, or by shipyard workers who specialized in refrigeration. My job was to monitor the system to make sure it was functioning properly while we were at sea.

One of the duties the *Penobscot* sometimes performed was retrieving "dummy" practice torpedoes shot by destroyers off the coast of Long Island. The torpedoes floated to the surface and we used a crane to lift them onboard the fantail of the ship. Then we returned them to port to be reused.

Midway through one of those trips, the head cook came to the engine room door and shouted, "Hey, Yates! We need you in the kitchen! Now!"

I bounded up the ladder and followed him. "What's going on?" I questioned.

Chapter 9

Between Doldrums and Danger

Something's wrong with the freezer!" the head cook cried. "Everything's thawing out!"

He peered over my shoulder as I tried to troubleshoot the problem. "Can you tell what's wrong?" he asked nervously. "If this freezer goes down, all the meat will spoil and we'll be in big trouble!" He continued talking while I tried to concentrate on the problem.

The cook was right. I could see that the freezer had already begun to heat up. Our food supply *was* in jeopardy. "Well, the expansion valve seems to have failed," I told him after I'd checked everything. "It isn't feeding Freon into the freezer. I'm going to try to replace the expansion valve mechanism. That may solve the problem."

"Okay," he said. "I sure hope that makes it work!"

So did I!

But replacing the expansion valve didn't fix the problem. I knew it was possible to bypass the thermal expansion valve and meter the Freon by hand, if necessary. But it is very tricky to regulate. If the Freon is fed too slowly, the box will warm up and the meat could thaw and spoil.

But if it is fed too quickly, the liquid Freon will destroy the compressor—which would take down both the freezer and the vegetable cooler.

I went to the engineering officer to explain what was happening, and told him I was going to try to meter the coolant myself. "Okay," he said, "but I can't help you. You're going to have to do the best you can and get rest when you can. I'll have a technician from York meet the ship when we return to port."

For the next four days I spent about 20 hours each day standing in the refrigeration room watching the freezer thermometer and several gauges, along with listening to the compressor. That left only four hours total, in short spurts, to get any rest.

One day, when I was bleary-eyed from endless hours of adjusting the Freon, one of the sailors came running into the refrigeration room and shouted, "Yates, come up topside! You gotta see this!"

I shut off the valve and followed him up to the deck. There was a commotion on the fantail and I squeezed my way through the sailors to see what was happening. I could hardly believe my eyes.

Since the deckhands hadn't seen any dummy torpedoes to retrieve yet, and were quite bored, one of them decided to go deep-sea fishing. He managed to catch something on his heavy line, but he couldn't get it reeled in. Another deckhand finally used the on-board crane to help haul a massive 20-foot shark onto the fantail. The sailors thought they'd killed it, but the shark was still very much alive. Every time one of them got too close, it would lash out—nearly catching them in its snapping jaws.

As I watched, they used the crane to lift the huge creature back into the water. I just shook my head as I started below deck. At least it had been a diversion from the tedium of keeping the freezer properly cooled.

When we finally got back to port, the technician from York Corporation wasn't there, so I had to continue the routine even though I was extremely exhausted. The engineering officer said, "I'll put a call in for shipyard workers—if you think they can help you.

"I believe it's a faulty stop-valve—just ahead of the expansion valve." I told him. "I think it is closed, but since it's soldered in place, I can't remove it. They'll need to empty the system of Freon before working on it."

The shipyard workers removed the split-stem valve and found that it was corroded and stuck closed. They changed the valve, replaced the coolant, and checked the system for leaks. It worked perfectly.

"You did a good job of diagnosing the problem with the freezer, Yates," the engineering officer said, giving me a rare compliment. "Now you'd better hit the sack!"

"Yes, Sir. Thank you, Sir," I said as I headed off to bed. I was *so* glad to get into my bunk! I slept for the next 24 hours.

A few months later, in October 1954, we were tied up alongside the pier in Brooklyn Naval Shipyard when the captain received orders to proceed again to Mayport Basin in Florida. We were to pick up a barge loaded with live ammunition and deliver it to Rhode Island. Most of the barges we towed were almost as long as our ship, and some were even wider.

It took several days to reach Mayport Basin, since our top speed was only 12.6 knots (about 14.5 miles per hour). There we attached the woven steel towline to the barge. The towline, which was about 2½ inches in diameter, fed through a pulley system. From there two cables split off like a "Y" with one end attached to each side of the barge. Once the barge was secure, we headed down the canal and back out to sea.

The water was fairly calm when we first started north. The captain knew a storm was approaching, but he must have felt there was no real danger. He couldn't have been more wrong!

Toward the end of the second day as we headed north, the wind picked up and the seas became rougher. In boot camp we'd learned that the wave heights in the ocean are measured by "states." State 0 means the sea is as smooth as glass. State 1 is a little choppy. In states 2-4 the waves are progressively larger. And state 5 waves are 40 feet high from trough to peak—about the height of a four-story building.

By the third day we were in State 5 waves, and I learned this was part of Hurricane Hazel, traveling on a direct line toward New Jersey and up into New York State. Even though we were going full speed, we bounced around like a cork in the ocean and made no headway. The waves caused the barge to double back on our ship. Once I peeked out on deck, looked up, and saw the barge on top of a wave directly above our ship. I gasped in terror! The barge was large and heavy. If it landed on our tugboat, we would sink. No one talked about it, but I saw the same fear in everyone's eyes.

We were opposite the New Jersey shore when the captain made the decision to turn the barge loose, and try to maneuver away from it before it destroyed us. "Cut the cable!" he shouted. The towing mechanism contained a cable cutter, which in an emergency could cut the cable in one quick motion. We had no idea where the barge of live ammunition would end up, or if it would do any damage once it was freed. It could be dangerous for some other vessel. However, most ships that are not anchored at a dock usually head to sea to ride out storms in the open ocean. We could only hope other ships were either far out at sea, or else safely in port.

After cutting the barge loose we headed as fast as possible in close to the shore, and then up the coast toward our home port in Brooklyn. When we finally tied up at our own berth, I breathed a huge sigh of relief and felt my tense muscles finally relax.

The winds were relentless even after we docked. I was worried about my mother and step-father who lived in Varna, just outside of Ithaca, New York. Since I had liberty that weekend, I decided to hop in my old Ford and buzz up there to make sure they were okay. When I started out, the eye of the storm was over central New York. But by the time I reached their home a few hours later, it had moved eastward toward New England. I made it to Varna and found my family had sustained no damage from the storm, which had passed just east of

Ithaca. It was very unusual for hurricanes to make landfall in the northern states. This was the only one I'd ever heard about at that time. I hoped we'd never have to be at sea again in that type of weather! Later I learned that the barge ended up on the southern shore of Long Island, where it was retrieved by different navy tug.

Another cold winter day our assignment was again to proceed to Mayport, Florida, to tow a YTB (Yard Tug Big) that was to be recommissioned to Quonset Point, Rhode Island. We headed south and carefully made our way up the narrow man-made canal to Mayport Basin. The YTB was almost as long as our 130-foot ship. After we'd attached the tow cable, we headed back out to sea. As we proceeded north in the Gulf Stream, the crew regularly checked to make sure the tugboat was secure.

Life aboard the *Penobscot* seemed to alternate between mind-numbing boredom, and life-threatening danger. When we were on duty while at sea, time often dragged—especially during the wee hours of the morning. Early on the third day after we picked up the YTB, I was on duty in the engine room trying to keep myself awake, when the scream of the general alarm suddenly jolted through the ship.

Chapter 10

Aboard a Sinking ship

Just as the light began to dawn on our third day of towing, the helmsman on duty glanced back toward the tow and was shocked to see the YTB was almost entirely submerged. As he sounded the alarm, the captain and our entire crew scrambled up on deck. In paralyzed astonishment we gazed at the sinking tug—knowing that if the YTB sank it could take our ship down with it! The shock was quickly replaced by action as the captain barked out commands. He sent out an SOS signal, cut the engine, and then reeled in the huge yard tugboat close beside our ship.

We hooked up pumps to get rid of the seawater that filled the tugboat. The wooden hull of the YTB was constructed of horizontal planks. Undoubtedly these had shrunk while it was in dry dock. Now water was flooding in—nearly sinking it.

While the P500 salvage pump droned, a destroyer escort ship several miles away picked up our distress signal and headed our way. A cold wind tore at us as we worked to rescue the tugboat. The pump labored all morning, but the water seemed to be pouring in faster than the pump could drain it. Finally, in the late morning, we used an on-board crane to pull our biggest pump, which was powered by a Model A car engine, out of the aft hold. The second class petty officer charged the battery and tried repeatedly, but unsuccessfully, to start it. In desperation he decided to drain the antifreeze-laden water out of the radiator and fill it with boiling water. When that was done the engine finally started with a bang and a puff of smoke. We quickly placed the six-inch-diameter suction hose into the YTB, threw the discharge line over the side, and began to pump the water from the tug's engine room. This time we made progress! As the water level went down, the tug rose slowly in the ocean.

About that time the destroyer escort arrived. They sent over a small dinghy manned by a young ensign and two other seamen. "What can we do to help?" they shouted as they slowed down, trying to keep the craft steady amid the swells.

"Nothing!" the captain shouted back. "We have everything under control now!" The men turned around and powered back through the waves toward their ship.

It was late afternoon before most of the water was finally pumped out, but seawater was obviously still pouring in. "It can't be coming in through the hull anymore," the first mate told the captain. "Those boards would have swollen up by now and sealed the gaps!"

The captain nodded. "There must be a leak somewhere else." Turning toward the waiting sailors he shouted, "I need a volunteer to board the boat and see what's wrong!" His plea was met by silence.

No one wanted to volunteer to board the disabled tugboat. Finally, reluctantly, I raised my hand. Quickly I was handed a battery-operated waterproof battle lantern. I swung over the side of our ship and climbed onto the deck of the tugboat. I could hear water gushing as I carefully descended the ladder. Holding the lantern high, I sloshed into the engine room. I couldn't see anything wrong along either side. I followed the sound of rushing water, and finally found the source. The two-inch pipe bringing water to cool the packing gland on the propeller shaft, had corroded and broken. No wonder our pumps couldn't keep up with it! I slogged back to the ladder, scrambled up on deck, and shouted to the watching sailors on our ship, "I need a damage control plug for a two-inch line, and a mallet to drive it home!" These were quickly lowered to me. I clambered back down into the engine room. As I pushed the wooden peg into the hole, a geyser of water sprayed out all sides, thoroughly drenching me. I held onto the plug as I swung the mallet and hit it squarely. The peg stayed in place, so I hammered it in tight. The leak stopped.

With the huge pump still running, I could see the water level immediately starting to recede. I breathed a sigh of relief as I gratefully climbed back onto our ship and headed below to change into dry clothes.

The water soon drained from the engine room of the YTB. Before untying the boat from our side, the captain decided to put a crew on the tug to make sure the plug held.

"I need a security crew onboard the ship!" the Captain shouted. This time no one volunteered, so he chose me, along with Metalsmith Clauson and Boatswain Mate Brown. He gave us a pot of strong coffee and some sandwiches, a small two-way radio for communication, and told us to stay on watch until we reached our destination.

Quickly the three of us scrambled over the side of our tugboat onto the deck of the disabled ship. Brown and I were good friends, but I didn't know Clauson as well. He hung around with the crowd that liked to hit the bars while we were in port.

Our ship jerked into motion as the *Penobscot* started up again and the tow line tightened. We settled in on the deck of the YTB as best we could in the bitter March wind, and drank coffee to keep warm. Every few minutes one of us went below deck to make sure there were no more leaks.

"So, Yates," Clauson asked, pulling his coat tightly around himself. "How'd you end up here?"

"The captain told me I had to!" I shot back, grinning.

Clauson laughed as he held his hands over the steaming coffee. "I mean why did you join the Navy, and how'd you end up on an ocean-going tugboat like the *Penobscot*?"

"Well..." I hesitated. "It's a long story."

Brown also urged me to tell them about my background. "So how *did* you end up here?"

I knew we'd probably be talking to keep ourselves awake for most of the night. So I began by telling them how I learned about World War II starting when I was just eight years old, and my experiences during the war. I shared how I was drafted into the Army when I was 19, and joined the Navy to avoid direct combat.

They laughed as I told them about the time I'd flooded the *Penobscot* when I first came onboard. When I was finished, they each shared their experiences in the Navy. We talked about the dangerous storms we'd been through, and told sea stories we'd heard.

It was 0300 before we finally arrived at Quonset Point, Rhode Island. We were so glad that our vigil would soon be over! We waited for the two-way radio communication telling us we could reboard the *Penobscot*.

Meanwhile, our captain radioed the base captain and asked him to send someone out to get the tug. The base captain was not happy about being awakened from a sound sleep. He roared, "I am NOT going to wake up a crew and send them out at this hour!"

Our captain yelled back, "Well I'm NOT going to wait around until morning to deliver this ship!"

After more heated words were exchanged, the base captain shouted, "I don't care *what* you do with it!"

"Okay then, you can come retrieve it from Brooklyn!" our captain bellowed, and hung up. He gave the order to head back to our home port.

Suddenly our two-way radio came to life. "We're not dropping off the YTB tonight. You're going to have to stay aboard until we get back to the base."

Brown grabbed the radio and shouted, "Aye aye, Sir!" We all groaned. The coffee and sandwiches were gone. But the biting wind continued as we headed toward home.

The sun was just coming up when we finally reached our base. The three of us on the YTB were cold and cramped, and *very* glad to take hot showers and crawl into our own warm bunks to sleep the rest of the day.

I never found out what happened to the YTB. I assume the captain at Quonset Point eventually sent one of his own tugs to haul it back to their base. I was just glad the YTB hadn't taken us and our ship down with it!

Shortly after our experience with the sinking YTB, we got word that it was time to bring our ship into dry dock. The navy schedules each ship to be cleaned and repaired every two or three years. It is floated into a special enclosure, the entrance is closed, and all the water is pumped out. The ship settles onto large blocks. Then the barnacles are chipped off, the hull is sandblasted and repainted, the engines and pumps are overhauled. Any other necessary repairs are performed before the ship is returned to service. Dry dock for our tugboat was in Staten Island.

The captain announced that he needed someone to update the machinery history cards. "Who knows how to type?" he asked. I was the only one who raised my hand. He motioned for me to follow the chief engineer. I had no idea where we were going.

Chapter 11

This is the Life!

The chief engineer opened the door to the officer's stateroom and motioned me inside. "It's all yours!" He smiled as he indicated a comfortable chair and a desk, which held a manual typewriter and large file box.

"Each piece of equipment has a history card," he explained. "It tells when the part was installed on the ship, the hours of usage, any problems, and any maintenance that's been performed. Your job will be to check the serial numbers on each one, and type in all the notes. If you have any questions, you can check with me."

"Thank you, Sir! I will, Sir." I saluted as he turned to leave.

I was familiar with the box on the desk. It was the one where we kept notes about the repairs we made on specific equipment. I sat down, adjusted the chair, and closed my eyes. I could hear scraping and hammering already coming from the hull of the ship. I leaned back with a sigh and thought, *Ah! This is the life!*

I smiled as I recalled that I'd been just 15 years old

when I sat nervously in front of the stern-faced vice-principal at Ithaca High School. Silently he reviewed the transcripts from my previous school which were spread across his large mahogany desk. "Where are your math grades? I don't see any math classes here!"

Timidly I replied, "I haven't taken any, Sir." I'd completed elementary school in just six years. I enjoyed arithmetic. But during my first three years of high school in Liverpool, New York, I'd avoided taking any math classes—especially algebra. Seeing letters replacing numbers looked impossible to me. Just before starting my senior year in high school, I moved to live with my mother in Ithaca, New York, the home of Cornell University. Because it was a university town, the standards at that time in Ithaca High School were much higher than those in Liverpool.

The vice-principal, in his three-piece suit, sat very straight as he looked at me over the top of his glasses. "Well, we'll have to rectify that lack of math, won't we, Master Yates!"He scowled as he saw that I'd flunked history the previous year. "I think it would be best if you repeat your Junior year."

My voice squeaked as I answered, "Yes Sir!"

That year I signed up for Algebra and found that math wasn't so difficult after all! My math teacher, Miss Claflin, was the same teacher who had taught my mother when she was in high school. I pulled an A. My senior year I took Geometry and enjoyed that so much I wanted more math classes. So after graduation I decided to sign up for Algebra II during the following school year.

My mother suggested I also take typing. "Why?" I said. "That's just for girls."

"There are a lot of business opportunities for men who type," she said. "It isn't just for women." So, reluctantly, I signed up for typing class.

There were 23 girls in the class and only two boys. The other fellow soon quit. That left me alone with all those girls. They constantly razzed me about being the only boy in the class. It was very uncomfortable and I wanted to quit. But, with mother's encouragement, I decided to continue with the typing class.

I diligently practiced typing at home. It seemed to come naturally. When the finals came up in June 1951, the typing teacher announced that every mistake on the exam would take five points off our scores.

I made sure I got a good night's rest before the test. The next morning I did my best. When final grades were posted, I received the top grade in the class. The girls protested loudly. They were sure there must have been a mistake!

I turned 18 a few weeks before the end of that school year. I hadn't been sure whether typing was of any value or not. But as I sat in the cushy chair in the officer's stateroom and adjusted the typewriter, it was obvious I'd made the right choice!

If I hadn't known how to type, I would have spent the 3½ weeks in dry-dock doing dirty tasks, like crawling underneath the engines, and in the bilges. I was so grateful that my mother encouraged me to take typing!

The job of updating the history cards required quite

a bit of investigation. I searched out every piece of equipment on the ship, checked the serial number, and transferred all the data onto the finished cards. I actually enjoyed getting everything organized and up-to-date.

With the history cards finished, and the *Penobscot* newly repaired and repainted, we headed back to our berth in Brooklyn. Every evening after supper while we were in port, one of the sailors was responsible to pick out a 16mm movie that would be shown in the mess hall. Since there were around 30 enlisted men in the crew, each man had one day a month to select a movie. Most of the guys chose Westerns. John Wayne movies were favorites. No one ever picked a comedy, science fiction, a love story, or anything educational. I found it very boring to see the same type of movie night after night. When it was my turn, I selected something on the space program, a science fiction movie, or a comedy. The guys hated it, and I got teased about it. But I was determined to have a change of pace.

In our free time between watches, we had to find our own diversions to keep ourselves occupied. Sometimes we talked or played games. While we were at sea, men would often fish off the ship's fantail. The sailors delighted in putting hot sauce on pieces of bread and throwing it to the seagulls that followed our ship. When a bird caught the bread, it suddenly made a fast dive and flew low, with its bill skittering across the surface scooping water, trying to put out the fire!

While we were in port, some sailors visited their girlfriends. Others went sightseeing or shopping. One day while I was window-shopping in Brooklyn, I saw a ukulele for sale at a pawn shop. I'd learned to play a uke while in elementary school, so I thought it might be fun to have one onboard the ship. I bought it for a few dollars and spent many hours learning new chords and chord progressions.

On one warm sunny day in June, while I was off duty, Boatswain Mate Brown invited me to go for a ride with some of the boys in his flashy new convertible. We put on our dress blues and piled into the car. With the top down we turned up the radio as we went through the Lincoln Tunnel under the Hudson River and headed toward the New Jersey shore.

As we drove toward the ocean, we sang at the top of our lungs and waved at passing cars. When we reached the beach, we drove along the edge whistling at the sunbathers. Teenage girls seemed to be particularly attracted to men in uniform. When they responded positively to our wolf whistles and compliments, we'd shout, "Too young!" as we drove away laughing.

The girls would jump up and protest, "No we're not!"

We had no intention of picking up any girls; we were just a bunch of young fellows enjoying the beautiful day, having fun and letting off steam.

I wanted something more to do in my time off, so I finally got brave enough to take the dance lessons I'd paid for in Bermuda, at the Arthur Murray Dance Studio in Brooklyn. I started taking one lesson a week whenever we were in port. At first, I felt like I had two overly-large left feet, but gradually I became more comfortable. I learned to dance the waltz, then the tango, the foxtrot, the samba, the quickstep, and even the rumba. I would never be "a natural," as the salesman in Bermuda had predicted. But by the time I finished the lessons I felt confident enough to go with the guys to the USO dances, without fear of smashing some poor girl's feet! The next time I was off duty on Friday night, I put on my dress uniform and went with the other sailors to the USO in Brooklyn to try out my new skill.

I was standing by the snack table having some refreshments when a pretty, dark-haired girl approached me, introduced herself as Betty, and asked if I'd like to dance. I said,

"Well, I'm kind of new at it, but sure! I'll try." I didn't tell her I'd just finished taking dance lessons.

As I took Betty's hand and stepped out onto the dance floor, the band started to play a new song.

Chapter 12

A Beautiful Girl

As the band played a waltz, Betty and I glided easily around the floor. My confidence grew with each dance. Having this beautiful girl in my arms made all those Arthur Murray dance lessons worthwhile! After about half an hour, we decided to sit down. Betty was a wonderful conversationalist, so we talked the rest of the evening.

She asked me about my background, and wanted to know why I joined the Navy. Betty told me about her home in Oahu, Hawaii, and some of the things she enjoyed doing there. The hours passed quickly as we talked. At the end of the evening, she mentioned that a group of her friends came to her apartment on Saturday nights to play and sing Hawaiian songs. She said there were several fellows who played ukuleles, while the girls danced the hula.

"I learned to play the ukulele in grade school," I told her. "And I have a baritone uke with me on the ship!"

"Well," she said, "why don't you stop by my place on 125th Street in Manhattan, and join us any Saturday night you are free?" She wrote down her address and handed it to me.

On my next Saturday night off duty, I took my ukulele and rode the subway to her apartment. As I knocked on the door, I could hear the sounds of Hawaiian music wafting into the hallway.

Betty introduced me to her roommate, Jean, and to her other friends, most of whom were Asian. Jean had lived in Hawaii for several years, At first I just sat and listened as they sang a variety of Hawaiian songs, some in English, and some in Hawaiian. Since I play by ear, I was soon able to join in. The girls took turns dancing the hula to some of the songs. I went home with the haunting melodies echoing in my head.

I became a regular at Betty's on Saturday nights whenever I was off duty. I enjoyed the wholesome crowd she hung around with. One time they invited me to go with them to a Japanese restaurant. The food was delicious, but the only utensils were chopsticks. I tried to eat, but kept dropping the food. My new friends laughed and showed me how to hold chopsticks properly. It took lots of practice before I could get the food smoothly to my mouth.

After that Betty told me I was welcome to stop by her place any other evening that I had off, so I started going there regularly. Since Jean was often out with her boyfriend, Betty was lonely and enjoyed my company. We didn't go back to the USO dances on Friday nights. It was more fun just to sit in her comfortable apartment and talk. I was inexperienced with girls and shy, so it took me awhile to get up the nerve to kiss Betty. She liked kissing, but made it plain that nothing else would happen.

As I told her about my upbringing on a farm near Syracuse, New York, Betty expressed a desire to see the rest of New York State. Sometimes on weekends we drove out of the city to sightsee for a day.

"You know Lee, since I don't have a car—and you do—why don't we share expenses and take one weekend each month to go see more of the state?"

"I think that's a great that idea," I said, "but I don't know how I'll be able to pay my share. I can never seem to save any money."

"Well, why don't we open a joint savings account at the bank where I work," she said. "We can put aside funds for food and gas. I'll match anything you save, and we can deposit it in our account."

"Okay, I'll try," I agreed, hesitantly. "But I don't know how much I'll be able to contribute." But surprisingly, every two weeks when I got paid, I was able to save a bit toward our travels.

I modified my car seats so they would recline completely, and suggested we sleep in the car. That way we wouldn't have to pay for motel rooms. Because she trusted me, she thought that was a great idea.

Betty was homesick, so while we drove, we often listened to *Hawaii Calls* on the radio, which was broadcast live from Hawaii. The first weekend trip we took was to the Finger Lakes region of New York. We started out Friday after she got off work, and made it just past Binghamton, New York, before we decided to stop. We pulled off the road into an abandoned gravel pit west of Johnson City, and spent the first night sleeping in the car. It felt surreal to be sleeping innocently next to this beautiful girl. It took me a while to get to sleep.

The next day we drove up to Rochester, for the annual Azalea Festival. We had a wonderful time together and got back to the city late Sunday night.

The following month we made a trip to Niagara Falls. It was thrilling to stand, with my arm around Betty, so close to the massive, thunderous falls.

Another time Betty said she wanted to see *Santa's Workshop* at North Pole, New York. So we spent the weekend driving through the Adirondack mountains. We found the town of North Pole to be interesting—but really just a tourist trap. On our way back, we visited Fort Ticonderoga on the south end of Lake Champlain, and came home full of sunshine.

Being with Betty felt like the most natural thing I'd ever done. She was very bright and fun to be with. I'd never met a girl like her. I started spending most of my off-duty time with her.

One day Betty told me excitedly that her mother was coming to visit from Hawaii. "I've told her a lot about you, and she wants to meet you!" she said.

The following Saturday when I got off at noon, I showered, put on my dress uniform, and headed to her apartment. I wanted to make a good impression with her mom. It was mid-afternoon by the time I got there.

Betty's mother was part native Hawaiian, and part Portuguese. Her husband was an Air Force serviceman.

They had already eaten, but Betty brought out some special food they'd saved for me. First, they gave me Laulaus—pork wrapped in tea leaves, then in luau leaves, and roasted. I unwrapped it and found it to be delicious. Then came Lomi Lomi salmon—lettuce, finely chopped celery, onion, and raw salmon in some kind of dressing. That was also excellent. After I'd finished, Betty said excitedly, "I have something else for you to try!" She went to the refrigerator and pulled out a bowl. She didn't tell me what it was, but it looked like chocolate pudding. They sat and watched to see my reaction. I *love* chocolate pudding, so I dug in and put a big spoonful in my mouth. Then I froze. It tasted like cold liquid steel! Seeing the shocked look on my face, they both laughed.

Through a mouthful of the horrible stuff, I said, "What *is* this!?"

"It's poi," Betty said. "It's a staple in Hawaii."

Well, it tastes like it's made out of staples, too! I thought.

"What is poi?" I asked as I valiantly tried to swallow the disgusting mass.

She told me it was a root vegetable that is beaten smooth. The more it is broken down, the mushier it becomes. Her mother explained that poi is traditionally eaten with fingers, and it is referred to as one-finger poi, two-finger poi, or three-finger poi, based on how thick it is. Perhaps if I hadn't been expecting chocolate pudding, I might not have reacted so adversely.

Betty's mother had a pleasant personality. Like Betty, she was very easy to talk with. We spent the rest of the afternoon talking and laughing. I could tell she would be a lot of fun to be around, and I hoped I'd made a favorable impression on her.

After her mother's visit, Betty talked more and more about how much she missed Hawaii. One day when we were alone, she was very quiet—which was unusual for her.

"What's bothering you, Betty?" I asked. "You're never this quiet!" Betty and I always talked freely about anything and everything. She was an upbeat person who was never moody. I knew something must be very wrong.

Chapter 13

What Now?

Betty and I were sitting on her living room couch together with my arm around her shoulders. She had been so quiet that I finally pulled her to me and gently asked, "What's going on, Betty? What's bothering you?"

She immediately stood up and started walking back and forth from one side of the room to the other. It was obvious she had something very important on her mind and was trying to think of the best way to say it. I waited as she paced. I had a feeling it was somehow connected to her mother's visit.

Finally she sat down next to me again, and looked deeply into my eyes. I could see she was trying to hold back tears, so I took her hands in mine. Taking a big breath, she said, "Lee, I've decided to move back to Hawaii. And I think we should break off our relationship. There is no future for us!"

I was dumbfounded. I felt like I'd been punched in the gut. It was difficult to breathe. I had thought of Betty as a wonderful friend. But suddenly I realized that she was far more than a friend—I was very much in love with her!

Taking her in my arms, I asked, "Betty, will you marry me?"

"Lee, we are too different!" she cried, pulling away. Tears began to course down her cheeks. "I'm Catholic," she said, "and you're a Protestant. I want to raise my children Catholic. I plan on living in Hawaii, and you've never even been there! You might not be happy there."

"But I love you, Betty and I can't bear the thought of losing you. You're everything I've ever wanted in a wife!"

"I love you too, Lee. But love is not enough!"

"But we get along so well together, Betty! I'm sure we can work out our differences. I'd be happy to live in Hawaii, if that's where you want to live."

"No," she said, brushing away the tears. "We need to stop seeing each other."

Nothing I said made any difference. I tried to reason with her. I pleaded. I cajoled. But it didn't help. She got up and went into her bedroom, then came out with cash. She showed me the bank statement from our joint savings account, and handed me half the money. Betty had obviously thought this through and made up her mind. She was adamant that our relationship was finished.

Devastated, I finally left. On my way back to the ship I stopped at a phone booth, called my mother, and poured out my broken heart. I had taken Betty to meet her on one of our weekend trips around New York State. The two of them had hit it off instantly. I told my mother the reasons

Betty had given for breaking up with me.

Mother was quiet for a moment, and then said, "You know, Lee, I think she's right! I know you care for her, but there are too many factors against you in this relationship." We talked about it for a few more minutes before we hung up. I trusted my mother's judgment, and did not pursue Betty anymore. By Christmas, Betty, my first love, was gone.

After that, whenever I had liberty, I didn't know what to do with myself! I'd been going to Betty's place for almost a year, and it had become second nature. Instead, I walked the streets, looking absently in shop windows. One day I noticed a beautiful silver King Zepher saxophone in a pawn shop window. I wondered if it played similar to a clarinet. In high school my mother had given me a used clarinet for Christmas, and I had taught myself to play. I'd even played in the school band.

I went inside the shop and found the saxophone was dirt-cheap because the whole instrument needed to be re-padded. I bought it for a song, and took it back to the ship. At a music store I found a repadding kit and a book on how to play the saxophone.

I dismantled the instrument and spread the parts out over my bunk. Looking at all the pieces, I wondered if I'd ever be able to get it put back together properly! It took several hours, but when the last part was in place, I blew a clear mellow note. The saxophone worked perfectly. I got out the book and started to learn how to play.

Soon I was able to play any song by ear, as well as some songs by note. One of the other sailors on our ship heard me playing and stopped to listen. He told me that he and some friends played at a bar in town. He suggested I join them. I agreed, and the next time I had a Saturday night off, I went with him to the bar. It was fun to play the current tunes for the customers. Periodically someone would buy us a beer. I'd never drunk much alcohol because I didn't like the taste. But I thoroughly enjoyed playing with the group. It also kept me from missing Betty so much.

During my time off, I started doing more sightseeing. I wandered around Times Square, went to the top of the Empire State Building, and skated at Rockefeller Plaza.

One day when I was walking along the docks, I saw the beautiful Italian luxury liner *SS Andrea Doria*. I struck up a conversation with one of the workers and told him I was an engineman on a tugboat. I mentioned that I'd love to see their engine room. Since I was in uniform, he offered to show me around the ship. We toured the formal dining room, the ball room, several cabins, and finally the engine room. He told me they had the capacity for 1,200 passengers and 500 crew members. It was very impressive and a good distraction from my grief over losing Betty.

A few months later I heard that the *SS Andrea Doria* had collided with a Swedish ship off the coast of Massachusetts. Struck in the side, the top-heavy *Andrea Doria* immediately started to list severely to starboard, which left half of its lifeboats unusable. The ship stayed afloat for several hours. Other ships responded, and over 1,600 passengers and crew were rescued. But 46 people died.

The following morning the luxurious ship capsized and sank. I was shocked. And to think I'd been aboard that beautiful ship only a few months earlier!

I continued to keep myself as busy as possible when I was off duty, and I welcomed our trips out to sea. Someone told me the USO on Lexington Avenue in Manhattan,was giving out free tickets for Broadway shows. I stopped by there regularly while we were in port, to pick up tickets. I went to see several Broadway shows, including the Rockettes, as well as some radio programs. I never went back to the USO dances. It hurt too much. I still ached for Betty.

Since my four-year enlistment was almost over, I began to formulate plans for the future. Basically, I had two choices. I could reenlist and consider making the navy a career, or get out and go to college on the GI Bill benefits. At that time, the navy would pay for four years of college. I thought it might be wise to get out of the navy, and go to school somewhere far away from New York City—and all the reminders of Betty. But then suddenly, a new opportunity presented itself.

Chapter 14

An Opportunity

Just before Christmas, 1955, I was in the engine room in the late afternoon when the ship's clerk, Personnelman Kenneth Brazier, called down from the top of the engine room ladder and said, "Hey Yates, it's your turn to pick the flick."

He grinned down at me as I started up the ladder, and said, "I know what kind of movie you're going to get. And it certainly won't be a Western!"

"By the way, Yates," Brazier said as I climbed onto the mess hall landing, "did you see the announcement I had pinned up on the refrigerator in the mess hall about the new navy rating called "Guided Missileman Training Program?" You're different from most of the guys, and pretty sharp. That might be right up your alley."

"I didn't see it," I replied. "Can I take a look at it?"

He scratched his head, "It was posted for several weeks. I'll see if I can dig it out of the files and let you look at it."

I waited while Brazier went into his office, which was just off the mess hall. Within a minute he returned. "I found it!" he proclaimed, handing me the rumpled paper.

I scanned the list of qualifications. It said the applicant must not have any disciplinary actions, civilian problems, or crimes on their record. *Well, I don't,* I thought. They must be a citizen. *I am.* There were to be no ties to any foreign adversary—for themselves or anyone in their family. *There aren't.* Academically they had to have a score of at least 110 for a combination of their math and GCT (general classification test—basically an intelligence test). *My scores are much higher than that. No problem. I meet all these requirements!* The new rating would also require a U.S. Government Secret Security Clearance.

I considered my options. By that time, I had attained the rank of Engineman Second Class (E5). I enjoyed my work, but there wasn't much room for advancement. With this new training I might be able to get into a brand-new program learning about guided missiles. I knew this would undoubtedly be a big part of the future in the military. They said that if I qualified, I'd be sent to school and given a full education in electronics—the same level of electronics schooling that a navy electronics technician was given. That appealed to me. I'd really wanted to understand electronics ever since the time I blew up the meter in the engine room.

Weighing this new opportunity against a four-year college education was a tough decision. After much thought, I decided to put aside college for the time being. I could always go later. This new training sounded like a great opportunity for me. Plus, I'd be able to get away from the New York City area—and all reminders of Betty.

Personnelman Brazier sent a letter (signed by the Captain) attesting to my exemplary military performance and good character; requesting that I be allowed to transfer into the new guided missile program. After a few weeks the Bureau of Naval Personnel responded—I was approved to enter the 20-week C-School Electronics Training in Treasure Island, California, subject to my obtaining a U.S. Government Secret Security Clearance.

Applying for the Secret Security Clearance took over two months—and piles of paperwork. During the process, the military interviewed my previous employers in Rochester, New York, my friends, former neighbors, and teachers—even my elementary school teacher, Miss Drohan!

In the spring of 1956, I finally received my Secret Security Clearance, and finished up the application for guided missile school. Within a month I received word that I'd been accepted into the newly-formed rating—which meant that I had to re-enlist for another six years. In late April, I received orders to report to Treasure Island Naval Training Center in California, in the first part of July.

I didn't have a decent car to travel with. I still had my old Ford clunker, and I wasn't sure it would make it across the country. With my shipping-over (reenlistment) bonus of $1,200, I decided to get a new car. I went to the local Ford dealer and put money down on a brand-new ivory-and-black 1956 Ford Customline. It was a beautiful car! I still had a few extra dollars from my bonus to pay for car insurance.

Since I had accumulated around 30 days of leave, I

decided that when the time came, I'd drive to the west coast and sightsee along the way. In the meantime, I babied that car, carefully changing the oil regularly, and keeping it washed and polished. I drove up to my mother's house to show it off.

One weekend while I was still on the ship, my friend Sparkey invited me to ride with him in a car he'd borrowed, to visit his girlfriend in Washington, D.C. He was a good driver and we had a nice weekend.

"You know, Sparkey," I said, on our way back to the ship, "you are welcome to borrow my car anytime, if you'd like to. I know you'll be very careful." I knew he made monthly trips to see his girlfriend.

Several weeks later Sparkey planned to take a bus out to the highway and hitchhike to D.C. It was raining, so I suggested he take my car.

"No! No!" he said. "I don't want to borrow your new car. I couldn't do that!"

"I've got to stay onboard ship this weekend, anyway, and won't need my car," I said, holding out my car keys. "You're a good driver, and I trust you. So you're welcome to borrow it." Sparkey thankfully accepted the keys and told me he'd be especially careful.

Sunday afternoon I got a call from him. He was still in Maryland. "Yates, you have insurance on your car, right?"

I gripped the phone receiver tighter as I said, "Uh … yes..."

"What company?" he asked.

Panic began to rise in my throat!

Chapter 15

An Accident and a Girl

Hardly daring to breathe, I rasped into the phone, "What's going on, Sparkey?"

"Well … I had this accident," he started to speak rapidly, as if he wanted to get it over with as fast as possible. "I was headed north, and a farmer was ahead of me. He realized he'd almost passed his turn, and stomped on the brake. I had to drive off the road to avoid hitting him." Sparkey paused for a moment, and then continued more slowly. "And it rolled the car, Yates. It ended up on its top!"

"Are you okay?" I asked.

"Yeah, I'm fine. The windows were down, so I crawled out. But the car's badly beat up. I'm soooo sorry!"

"Where is it now, Sparkey?"

"I had it towed to a Ford garage near here. They're waiting for permission to start work on it. I really am sorry about the accident, Yates!"

"It's okay, Sparkey. I'm glad you weren't hurt!"

I *was* very thankful my friend hadn't been injured—

but also devastated to think my new car had been so severely damaged.

Sparkey hitchhiked back to the ship. He told me again how terrible he felt that he'd wrecked my new car. But I assured him I held no grudge. I was the one who insisted he take my car on his trip. The accident could have happened to anyone.

Shortly after Sparkey returned, my tour of duty on the *U.S.S. Penobscot* came to an end. I said goodbye to my friends, and then I took a bus to Maryland to survey the damage on my car. I arrived on Saturday afternoon and found an inexpensive rooming house not far from the Ford garage. Walking around the area, I saw a diner where I could eat supper cheaply. I wasn't sure how long the car repairs would take, and wanted to conserve my funds as much as possible.

The next morning I attended a nearby church. After the service I complimented the minister, Reverend Whitehurst, on his sermon. He thanked me, and since I was in uniform, he asked me about myself, and how I happened to be there. I told him briefly of my new assignment in California and about my car.

"Where are you having lunch?" he asked.

"I went to the diner near the rooming house last night," I replied. "I'll probably get some lunch there."

"They're closed on Sunday," he said. "In fact, I doubt that you'll find any place within walking distance open today. Why don't you join my wife and me for lunch?"

I was delighted to accept his kind invitation. When everyone left, Reverend Whitehurst closed up the church, and we walked together to their lovely home just a few doors away. Mrs. Whitehurst had prepared a delicious meal.

After lunch Reverend Whitehurst invited me to sit with him in their back yard. We talked about gardening, and he asked me more about myself and my background.

"By the way," he said, "our teenage daughter, Jan, is at a friend's house today. She'll be home this afternoon. Tonight we'll be taking her to go boating with some friends at a lake near here. You are welcome to come along and ride with us if you want to. I think you'd enjoy the group. They're a lot of fun."

Jan came home just before suppertime. She was a pretty girl with big blue eyes and a beautiful smile. She seemed friendly, but a bit reserved. We spent some time talking, and I decided to accept their invitation and go on the outing with them. I thought it might give me a chance to become a little better acquainted with Jan.

That evening, after discussing it with his wife, Reverend Whitehurst invited me to stay in their guest room while my car was being repaired. I gladly accepted. That was much better than paying for the rooming house! I picked up my things and took them to the Whitehurst's home.

On Monday morning Mrs. Whitehurst stopped me as I was about to leave for the Ford repair shop. "When will you be back, Lee?" she asked.

"Well, after I check on my car, I thought I'd look around town a bit."

"Why don't you plan on being here for supper at

6:00?" she asked.

"Okay, I'll do that! Thanks!"

At the repair shop I wanted to cry when I saw the shape my beautiful new car was in. Not a square yard had escaped damage. The fenders, doors, and top all needed to be repaired or replaced and repainted. I was told it would take several weeks to finish the car. It was a good thing I'd accumulated extra days of leave, plus 30 days of travel time!

As I left the repair shop and headed toward town, I passed a restaurant with a sign in the window that said, "PART-TIME DISHWASHER WANTED." I went in and talked with the owner, explaining that I was interested in the job, but I'd only be there for a few weeks. He was glad to have help, and I was happy to earn a little extra money. So I started that day.

When I finished washing dishes, I had lunch, and then hitchhiked out to the local airport. I'd always been fascinated with airplanes, and hoped someday to get a pilot's license. At the airport I spent some time leaning against a tree and watching the small planes taking off and landing. In the late afternoon I thumbed a ride back into town, and walked to the Whitehurst's home.

The next day after work and lunch, I went to the airport again. The airport manager saw me hanging around and came over to talk with me. I told him why I was in town. "I sure wish I could take flying lessons!" I said.

He thought for a minute, and asked, "Do you know how to ride a tractor and cut grass?" I assured him I did.

"Well, we need the runways cut. For every four hours

you spend cutting grass, I'll give you a half-hour flying lesson. How does that sound?"

"You've got a deal!" I replied.

During the weeks while I waited for my car to be repaired, I spent the mornings washing dishes, then after lunch I thumbed a ride to the airport and mowed the grass. The airport manager gave me several flying lessons.

I spent the evenings talking with the Whitehurst family and playing games. They took me with them wherever they went, including to a beach house in North Carolina for a few days. While we were there I got to know Jan a little better. I'd been very lonely since Betty left, so it was nice to spend time with a girl. Some afternoons we went to the beach, where Jan and I played in the bay. The Whitehurst's treated me like part of the family.

Finally, after almost a month, the work on my car was completed. It looked like new again—except I had the repair shop repaint it ivory and royal blue—instead of black. At last I was ready to head for California.

Mrs. Whitehurst fixed a special breakfast on the morning I left. Then the family walked me out to the porch. "We're sorry to see you go, Lee," Reverend Whitehurst said, reaching out to shake my hand. "We're going to miss you."

"I'm going to miss you, too!" I said. "I've really enjoyed my time with you and your family. Thank you for all your kindness and hospitality." Mrs. Whitehurst and Jan each gave me a hug.

I swung my duffel bag up on my shoulder and turned

to Jan, "Why don't you walk me to my car?"

Jan smiled her beautiful smile and quickly followed me down the front steps.

I put the duffel bag in the trunk, got in the car, and rolled down the window. "Would you consider writing to me?" I asked.

"Sure!" she agreed. "I'll write to you every day, if you want me to."

"I'd like that! Your father has my address. And I will start writing to you every day on my trip to California."

"I'll be watching for your letters!" she said. Then she turned swiftly and ran back to the porch. I started my car, waved a final time, and headed west.

As I drove, I thought about Jan. *She is young ... but she seems very nice. She's from a delightful family ... and she's pretty. I wonder if she really will write to me every day? What can I write to her about? Will I end up falling for her, like I did for Betty?*

Chapter 16

Travel Troubles

On my trip across the country, I tried to drive 500-600 miles each day. Motels often advertised their rates on billboards, so I was able to find inexpensive lodging. Most of the places I stayed were very simply furnished, but reasonably clean.

I had traveled up and down the Eastern Seaboard of the United States, but I'd never been west of Pennsylvania. It was fun to see the differences in topography. Knowing I'd be writing to Jan at the end of each day made me more aware and watchful.

I enjoyed the lush beauty of the West Virginia mountains, and was amazed by the miles and miles of flat cornfields in western Ohio and Indiana. Then on through Illinois to Missouri. In Hannibal, Missouri, I crossed the mighty Mississippi River, and stopped by Samuel Clemens' house. I knew Jan loved to read, and she'd probably read *The Adventures of Huckleberry Finn* and *The Adventures of Tom Sawyer*. I wanted to tell her what Mark Twain's home looked like. I didn't have time to stop and tour the inside of the house, because I hoped to get to

Treasure Island Naval Base a few days before my class started.

The western part of Kansas and eastern Colorado were mostly flat and dry. I'd heard so much about the beauty of Colorado that I was surprised to find it so bleak. But before long the beautiful snow-capped Rocky Mountains came into view. As I started to climb the eastern slope of the mountains my car kept going slower and slower no matter how much I pressed on the gas pedal.

I arrived in Colorado Springs in the afternoon. I'd planned to drive to the top of Pike's Peak, but because of my car problems, I thought it would be wise to stop at the Ford garage and have it checked. By then my car was going so slowly that I barely made it to the stoplight by the garage. I went inside and explained to the mechanic that my new car wasn't running properly.

He laughed and said, "You're from the East Coast, aren't you?"

"Yes," I said, "but how did you know?"

"It sounds like you have an East Coast car. Your carburetor needs to be adjusted in order to work at this altitude, and you need to add a fuel pump. I can do that for you. How long are you planning to be in this area?"

"I'm only staying overnight. I'm actually on my way to California," I said. "I was hoping to drive up to Pike's Peak."

"In that case, there's no need to adjust the carburetor or add a fuel pump. Your car will work fine once you get back down to a lower elevation. I suggest you take the cog railroad, or a limo to Pike's Peak. They don't cost very much."

It was a relief to hear there was no serious problem with my car! I settled into a nearby motel, and the desk clerk told me where I could get a limo to take me up the mountain. Early the next morning I arrived at the limousine service at the same time as an elderly couple. We introduced ourselves and decided to share the expense for the ride to Pike's Peak. It took about an hour to navigate the 150 switchbacks. The view at the top was incredibly clear. We could see for miles. But we didn't stay long, because it was difficult to get enough oxygen at 14,000 feet. We quickly climbed back in the limo and headed down the mountain.

As soon as the limousine deposited us back in Colorado Springs, I started out for New Mexico, and then on to Arizona, and the Grand Canyon. It was late at night before I finally arrived at the South Rim. Since there were no motels nearby, I pulled into a rest area, curled up in the back seat of my car, and slept fitfully.

The next morning I drove to the different overlooks of the Grand Canyon and enjoyed the majestic beauty of that mighty chasm. After that I headed north toward Page, Arizona, through southern Utah, and then on to Las Vegas, Nevada—where I planned to stay overnight prior to going through the Mojavi Dessert. As I traveled, I saw more and more cars with bags hanging on the front bumpers. At a small store where I stopped to get something to eat, I saw the same type of bags for sale. They were marked "water bags."

It was dark by the time I reached Las Vegas and the

city was awash in neon lights. When I stopped to fill up my fuel tank, the gas station attendant asked, "Where are you headed?"

"San Bernadino, California," I answered. "Any good places to sleep around here that aren't too expensive?"

"If you're going to San Bernadino, you'd better travel tonight and not tomorrow! Otherwise the heat will get you!" he said. "Do you have water bags?"

"No. I saw water bags for sale today. What are they for?"

"You'll need them when you cross the desert. Cars often overheat there, and people become stranded with no water. Even at night the temperature stays in the 90's this time of year."

I purchased two of the bags at the gas station, filled them with water, and hung them on my front bumper. They were made of tightly-woven canvas, which effectively kept water in, yet allowed the tiniest bit of moisture to seep to the outside. The breeze from the car cooled the bags until they felt like they'd been refrigerated.

After getting something to eat, I started my trek through the desert. I drove as fast as I dared. I didn't want to get stranded in the notorious heat.

Just as the sun was coming up, I reached San Bernadino. After stopping for breakfast, I removed the waterbags and emptied them, then took a short nap in the car. Even though I was very tired, I decided to head north toward Fresno.

As I drove, I could see they were constructing the new interstate highway just to the right of the freeway.

Although the traffic was heavy, it was moving at a steady pace. I kept glancing over and admiring the construction. Then suddenly as I looked back at the road, I saw brake lights. I slammed on my brakes—but not quickly enough! With a thud I hit the rear bumper of the car in front of me—which happened to be a Cadillac.

The driver of the Cadillac and I both pulled over on the side of the road. We got out and inspected our cars. It looked like there was no damage to his car except a scratch on one chrome bolt, but my front bumper didn't do as well. It was badly dented in the center.

I gave my information and new address to the other driver, and told him I'd pay whatever it cost. I didn't want the police involved, and I didn't want it on my driving record.

In Fresno I found a motel and went to sleep early. The next morning I made a quick trip to Sequoia National Park. I'd always wanted to see the giant Sequoias. After marveling at the massive trees, I left the park and headed toward San Francisco.

That evening, Wednesday, July 4, 1956, I drove across the Bay Bridge from Oakland toward San Francisco. I exited at Yerba Buena Island, and then on to Treasure Island, where I finally pulled into Treasure Island Naval Base.

School wouldn't start until the following Monday. So the next morning, I took the opportunity to remove the bumper from my car and stomped on it to straighten it. The dent popped out, and when I reattached the bumper it looked as good as new. Then I went to pick up my mail and found several letters from Jan waiting for me. I settled onto my bunk, sorted her letters by date, and read them. She was a really good writer. Corresponding with her was going to be fun! I hoped she'd been enjoying my letters, too.

On Friday, in addition to my daily letter from Jan, I received three other letters. The first was a bill for $35 from the owner of the Cadillac. I was glad to pay that and have it taken care of without any insurance involvement.

The second letter was from the collision insurance company. They'd paid my claim for repairing my car in Maryland. But because I was only 23, and I'd loaned the car out, and it had been in an accident, they were also cancelling my policy.

The third letter was from the liability insurance company. They told me that as long as I had a loan on the car, I was required to have collision coverage. They also tripled the price of my liability insurance.

I went to a pay phone and looked in the phone book for insurance companies. I called the first number listed. An insurance agent answered the phone.

"Hello, this is Lee Yates," I said. "I need to get collision insurance on a 1956 Ford Customline. Could you tell me how much that will cost?"

"Is your car licensed?"

"Yes. It's licensed in New York. But I drove out here, and arrived two days ago." I told him about my 20-week training at Treasure Island.

"Didn't you have collision insurance on your new car when you drove across the country?" I could hear a raised eyebrow in his tone of voice.

"Yes, of course!" I answered. "But my car was in an accident in Maryland, and the insurance company is canceling my collision."

"How old are you, Lee?"

"Twenty-three."

"Tell me about the accident," he said.

I told him about my friend Sparkey—who was an exemplary driver—and what had happened.

"Okay, give me a minute while I look up the rate and see what I can do for you." I heard him put down the phone and riffle through some papers. Finally he picked up the phone again. "Well, the best we can do, Lee, would be $300."

I gulped! "For a year?"

"No, that would only be for 6 months. Because of your age, and the fact that you loaned out your car, and had the accident, that's the best we can do. And I'm afraid it's the same rate any other insurance company is going to give you. Shall I write up a policy for you, Lee?"

I felt a shock run up my spine and I couldn't answer. I did not have that kind of money! Finally I swallowed and squeaked out, "No, not right now."

"Okay," he said. "Let me know if you want to go ahead with a policy."

I thanked him and hung up.

I was flabbergasted! There was no way I could pay that much for insurance. It was obvious I would not be able to keep my beautiful car. But I had to have a car to get around. And I needed to solve this problem before starting school on Monday—since my collision coverage would be running out in a few days. What could I possibly do?

Chapter 17

A New Adventure

I laid awake most of Friday night, tossing and turning, trying to decide how to solve my insurance problem. I *really* wanted to keep my car! I knew that if I took it to a car dealership, I'd lose money on it. I could try to sell it to an individual, pay off the loan, and with the extra money buy a cheaper car—but that would need to all happen in the next two days.

One other possibility was to trade my Ford for an older car. Then I'd only need liability insurance. If I could find someone with a good quality used car, they might be willing to trade and take over my car payments.

I felt more comfortable dealing with other sailors, instead of trying to negotiate with civilians. I believed I could trust navy men, and if there were problems, I'd be able to go to the military authorities to have any issues resolved. So after breakfast Saturday morning I went to the base personnel office and asked the clerk where most sailors with families lived in the area.

"That would be Alameda," he said. "It's close to the base, and there are whole sections of Alameda that have only navy families."

I spent the rest of the day washing and polishing my car, and cleaning out every speck of dust from the inside and the trunk. When I finished, it looked like it had just come off the showroom floor.

On Sunday I put on my dress uniform, and went to Alameda. There I slowly drove up and down the streets, looking for a car in reasonable condition that would be worth about as much as I had put into my car. I saw a sharp-looking 1950 Ford sedan parked in front of one house. It was polished to a shine and appeared to be well taken care of.

I pulled over and got out of my car. Slowly I walked around the vehicle. It looked good. So I strolled up the sidewalk and knocked on the door. When a man answered, I said, "How would you like a new Ford?"

He laughed. "Okay!" he said. "But what's the catch?"

"I still owe money on it and can't afford insurance. You let me have your car, and you take mine and pay it off."

He invited me in. We sat down in his living room and introduced ourselves. He was also a navy man. I told him of my background on the *U.S.S. Penobscot*, and my new assignment in the school at Treasure Island. Then I explained about the accident, which caused the insurance rates to escalate. He asked me more about my car, and how much I still owed.

"About $1,100,"

"Well, let's go take a look at it!" he said. We went

outside together. Since he was older, I knew he'd be able to get insurance much cheaper than I could. He walked around my car, and looked at the interior and the engine. "That's a beautiful car!" he said, stroking his chin in thought. Then he grinned and said, "Sure! Fine! I'll take it!"

Finally, I remembered to ask, "How does your car run?"

"Oh, it runs great!" he said enthusiastically, rubbing his hands together.

So we sealed the deal! We signed our car titles over to each other. I gave him the finance company paperwork, and I left with the shiny Ford sedan. I was happy, because with the older vehicle I only needed the cheapest liability insurance. But I missed my beautiful car and taped a picture of it to the inside my locker.

The next morning I woke up early, showered, got dressed, and went to the chow hall for breakfast. Then back to the barracks, where I picked up a notebook, pencil, and my trusty slide rule. My mind raced as I headed out the door. I was excited, but also nervous. I hadn't taken any classes since boot camp. I wondered how I'd do. Would I be able to understand and keep up?

I had some time before class started, so I decided to take a walk around the base to settle my nerves. The warm sea air coming off the bay felt refreshing. As I walked, I mulled over all that had happened during the last four years.

I thought of my carefree time living and working in Rochester, New York. And of the dreaded draft notice that sent me scurrying to the navy recruiter office. Then boot camp and working as a Recruit Educational Petty Officer, helping sailors in my company learn the material they'd been struggling with. Then being assigned to the *U.S.S. Penobscot*, and all that had transpired in the last four years.

There had been so many new experiences and adventures! I'd thoroughly enjoyed traveling to new places. There were some dangerous times—when I wondered if we'd survive the rough seas; and the time I was assigned to stay aboard the ship that had been sinking. I thought of the many friends I'd made, and of Betty and our year together—and the grief of losing her; then of getting my new car, the accident, and losing the car because of my irresponsibility in loaning it out; and recently of meeting Jan, and starting a friendship and correspondence with her. I wasn't sure where that might lead.

I wondered what my next duty station would be. After my new training I'd probably be assigned to a much larger ship. Where would I get to travel next?

The *U.S.S. Penobscot* had been my home for almost four years. It taught me responsibility in so many areas of my life. I was still a carefree teenager when I first climbed aboard the tugboat. There I received valuable training in working with engines and refrigeration systems, and learned many life lessons which helped me mature as a man. Then this new opportunity had opened up. It felt like I'd been led to this point in my life—like I was exactly where I was supposed to be.

With my thoughts settled, I turned my steps toward

the classroom. Several men were already there. More arrived in the next few minutes. The 21 students came from many different ratings: boatswain mates, fire-controlmen, gunner's mates, radiomen, and enginemen, like me. Textbooks were laid out on the tables. I opened the textbook in front of my chair. The many diagrams and symbols looked strange and complicated.

At exactly 0800 the doors opened and two chief petty officers entered the Guided Missiles Conversion Class. The chiefs introduced themselves, and told us to take a minute to greet our classmates.

The sailor to my right held out his hand, "Hi! I'm Frank Ramos."

"I'm Lee Yates," I said, shaking his hand.

"I noticed that you and I are only ones who have slide rules!" he said quickly. I nodded. Then we both turned to greet other people.

Next, the chief petty officers took muster (roll call). They explained what would be required of us, and told us we could expect this class to be fast-paced—with a lot of math included. A groan went up from some of the men. Frank and I glanced at each other and grinned, knowing that our slide rules were the best way to calculate any math problems. I thoroughly enjoyed math. Perhaps this class wouldn't be so difficult after all!

I opened my textbook to the required page—and began a whole new adventure!

—The End—

U.S.S. Penobscot ATA-188